EXOTIC ARTWORKS

RIPON DEY

ISBN: 978-1-7382691-5-0

Imprint: Shoily publisher.

Cover design by: ArtinApps

Library of Congress Control Number: 2018675309

Printed in the United States of America

EXOTIC ARTWORKS

Welcome to the captivating world of exotic artwork, a realm where imagination knows no bounds and creativity flourishes in its most vibrant hues. Within these pages, you will embark on a journey through the kaleidoscope of my artistic expression, where each stroke of the brush, each splash of color, and each intricate detail is a testament to the boundless wonders of the human imagination.

This collection is a celebration of diversity, encompassing a rich tapestry of themes, styles, and techniques. From the lush landscapes of distant lands to the mesmerizing allure of exotic fauna, each artwork beckons you to explore the depths of your own imagination and embark on a voyage of discovery.

Spanning across various mediums including oil painting, acrylic on canvas, watercolor, and sketches, this collection reflects my lifelong dedication to the craft of visual storytelling. Each piece is a labor of love, crafted with meticulous attention to detail and infused with a passion that knows no bounds.

In addition to showcasing my artwork, this book also offers a glimpse into the journey that has shaped my artistic vision. From my earliest inspirations to the evolution of my style, my hope is that this brief glimpse into my life will provide context and deeper insight into the creations that adorn these pages.

I am immensely grateful to the publisher for their support in bringing this collection to life and for including my biography at the beginning of this book. It is my sincere hope that this collection will not only inspire but also ignite a sense of wonder and curiosity in all who venture within its pages.

So, dear reader, I invite you to immerse yourself in the enchanting world of exotic artwork. Let your imagination take flight as you explore the myriad wonders that await within these pages. May this collection serve as a source of inspiration, joy, and endless fascination for years to come.

With warmest regards,
RIPON DEY

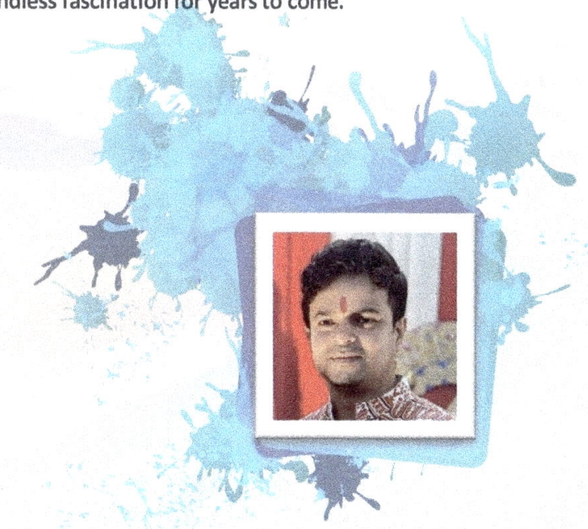

Contents

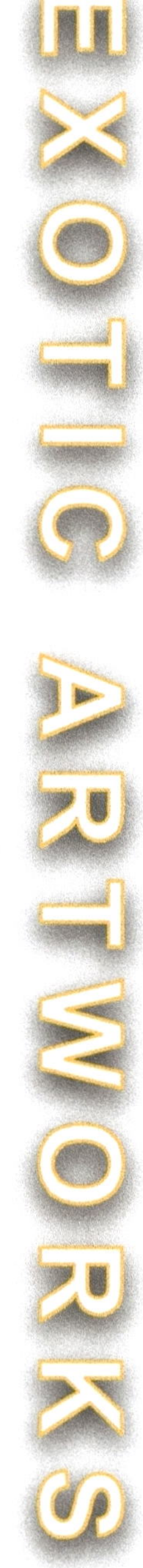

ARTISTS BIO AND BACKGROUND

Artistic Approach

Ripon's influences are, first and foremost, everything he sees, feels and experiences, but he has always loved comic books, particularly works by Harvey Pekar and Robert Crumb. He loves architecture, particularly Art Deco. The artists he most admires are John Martin, a mezzotint artist from the 1800's, Winsor McCay a cartoonist and animator who created Little Nemo, Escher; and Lyonel Feininger creator of Kinder Kids.

Notably, 70% of the money generated from his artworks will go to Non-profit organizations in Canada and Bangladesh. The rest will go to purchasing Artwork materials.

Bio.

Amateur artist from greater Vancouver in British Columbia. Ripon is a national-award winner from Bangladesh in Pencil Sketch and Watercolor category in 2002 organized by "Bangladesh National museum", Dhaka, Bangladesh. He does not set out to produce art about one subject to another.

Ripon's work tends to focus on the environment, the evolution of human being and natural wealth, the development of resources, more and more people, and the consequences this has on nature. Some reviews have labeled his work as 'black humour' but he always tries to depict a positive message too – the persistence of nature in recapturing what once belonged to the earth.

At school, the class he really paid an attention in was art. He simply thinks his obsession with depicting the monotony of the work place and work force started there.

Some of his subject matter is about people's daily routines and a comment on human nature. And since he has always been a fan of fine arts – a new strand of work seems to have emerged depicting a very 'human' and 'school playground' side to mob life.

None of it was intentional – it all developed and evolved over time. People always ask for his artist statement so he needed to do one but he has never liked to explain a certain piece of work – if you've made a picture and that's how you wanted it to be – hopefully it can speak for itself and whatever it says to the viewer – it's the right message because there isn't a wrong and a right message. Each person takes something a little different from the same picture and he is happy with that.

Juried and Non-Juried Exhibitions

1. Participated an exhibition titled "art without reservation" by the east west arts, Canada 2013 of contemporary arts by a group of 40+ Canadian and international artists at the Papermill art gallery from august 26th to September 16th 2013.

2. Participated "contemporary painting exhibition, 2011"venue: papermill art gallery, Toronto, Canada, number of participants: 12, duration: 31st may-13th June.

3. Participated "Annual Younger painting Exhibition" organized by Bangladesh Shilpakala Academy, Govt. of Bangladesh, 2001. Award: Best award on painting category.

4. Participated "10th Joint Youth Art Exhibition" organized by Shilpakala Academy, Govt. of Bangladesh, 1999.

5. Participated "9th Joint Youth Art Exhibition" organized by Shilpakala Academy, Govt. of Bangladesh, 1997.

6. Participated "Victory Day Art Exhibition" organized by Bangladesh National Museum, Dhaka, 1999. Award: Best artwork

7. Participated "Annual Art Exhibition" organized by SUPAN, Sylhet, 1999. Award: Best artwork.

Appreciation Award Obtained

1. Accorded National Award as a second position in the competition of Fine Arts organized by "Bangladesh National Museum", Shahbag, Dhaka in 1996.

2. Awarded as best artwork (Title: Still-life 2) in yearly art exhibition organized by Bangladesh Shilpakala Academy (Cultural Institute under Cultural Ministry of Bangladesh), Sylhet in 1999.

3. Awarded as best artwork in joint art exhibition organized by SUPAN, a reputed fine art education school, Sylhet in 1996.

4. Rewarded as 1st position in water color art competition from "Bangladesh Shishu Academy", Sylhet.

5. Rewarded as 1st position in pencil sketch art competition from "Bangladesh Shishu Academy", Sylhet.

6. Awarded as 2nd position in painting competition in regional level organized by Bangladesh Shilpakala Academy, Comilla.

7. Accorded felicitation certificate for overall fine arts performance organized by PLUS SERVICE, Sylhet and also have got many more awards in local art competitions.

Academic Qualifications

1. Two Years diploma program in Fine Arts from "Bangladesh Shilpakala Academy" (Cultural Institute under Cultural Ministry of Bangladesh), Sylhet.

2. Three years program in Fine Arts from "SUPAN"- a renowned fine arts education institute, Sylhet.

3. Served as a Fine art justice in a Art Competition organized by "Mahalaya Udzapan Parishad", Sylhet.

"contemporary painting exhibition, 2013" venue: papermill art gallery, Toronto, Canada, number of participants: 12, duration: 31st may-13th June.

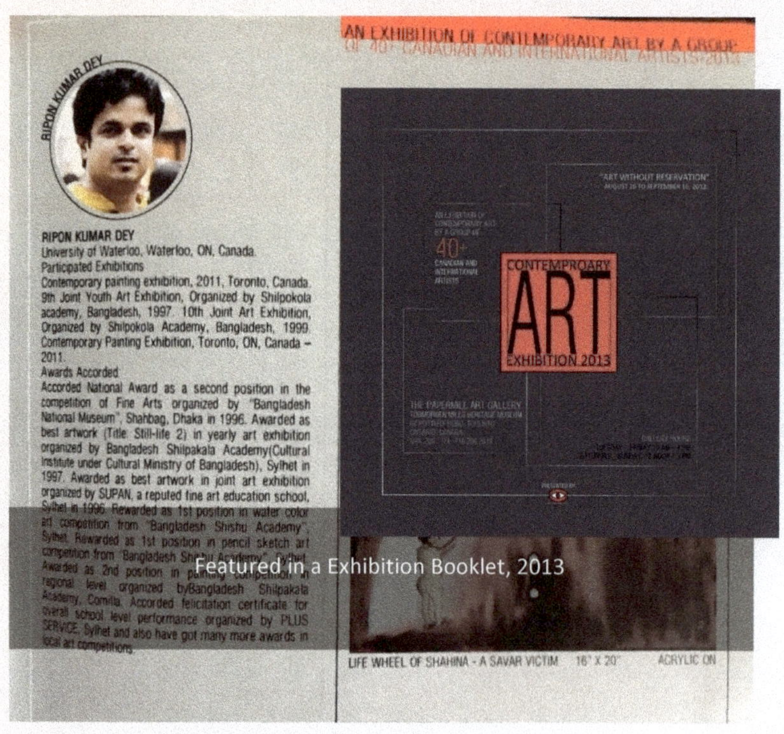

Featured in a Exhibition Booklet, 2013

"contemporary painting exhibition, 2011" venue: papermill art gallery, Toronto, Canada, number of participants: 12, duration: 31st may-13th June.

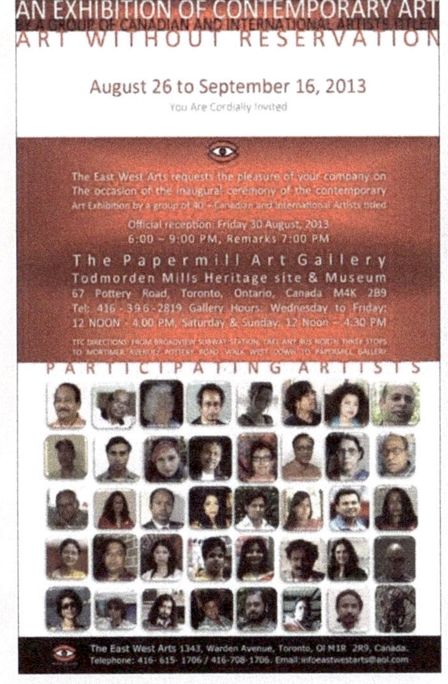

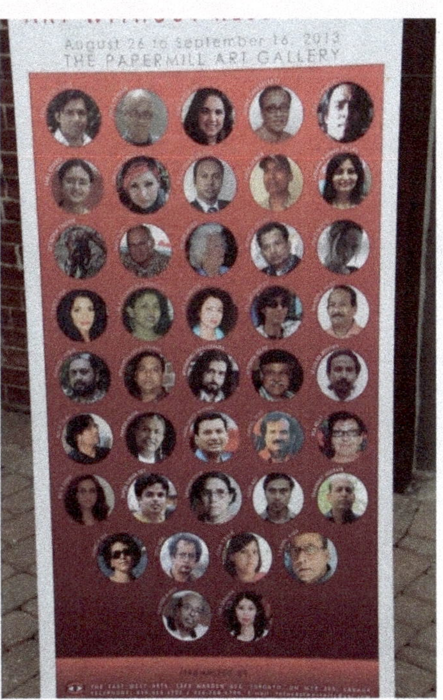

Participated in a painting exhibition in Toronto as a fine artist. This is an opening receptions brochure of "ART WITHOUT RESERVATIONS". A selected art exhibition by a group of 40+ Canadian & International artists at The Papermill art gallery in Toronto,Canada. 2013.

"contemporary painting exhibition, 2011" venue:
papermill art gallery, Toronto, Canada, number of
participants: 12, duration: 31st may-13th June.

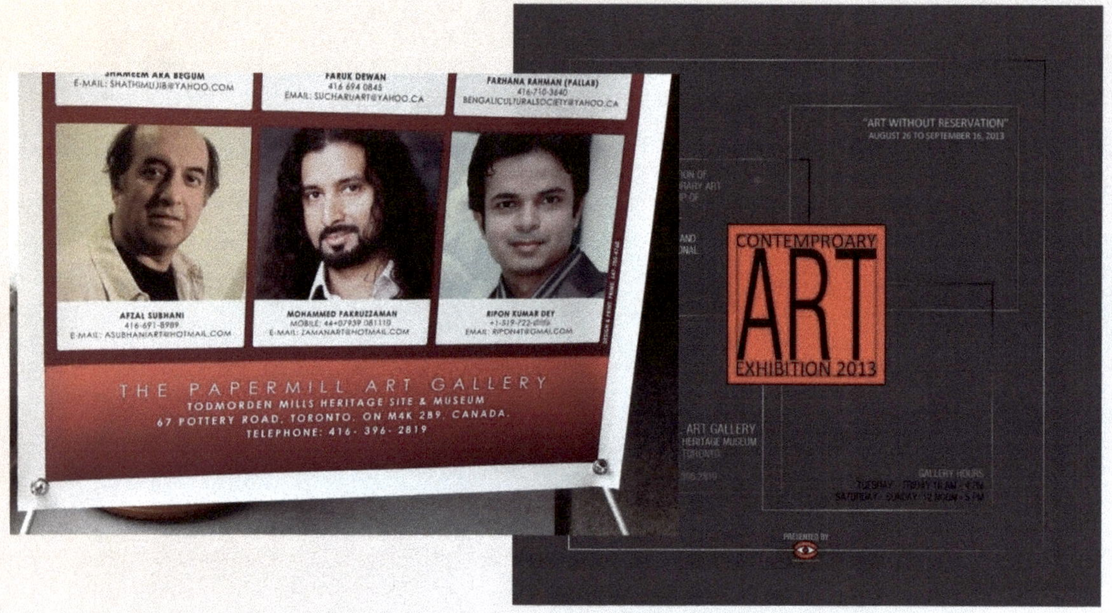

"contemporary painting exhibition, 2011" venue: papermill art gallery, Toronto, Canada, number of participants: 12, duration: 31st may-13th June.

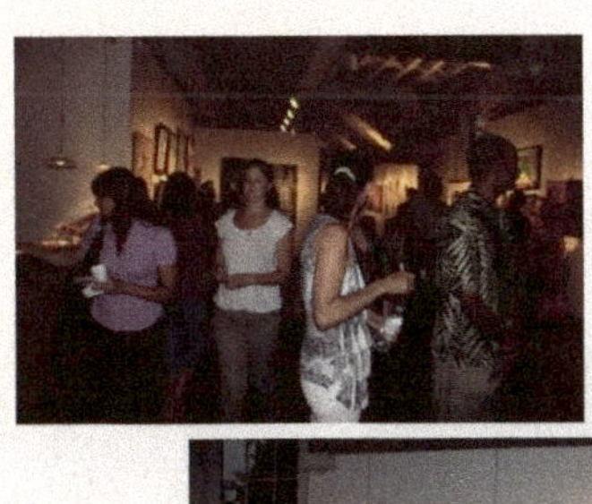

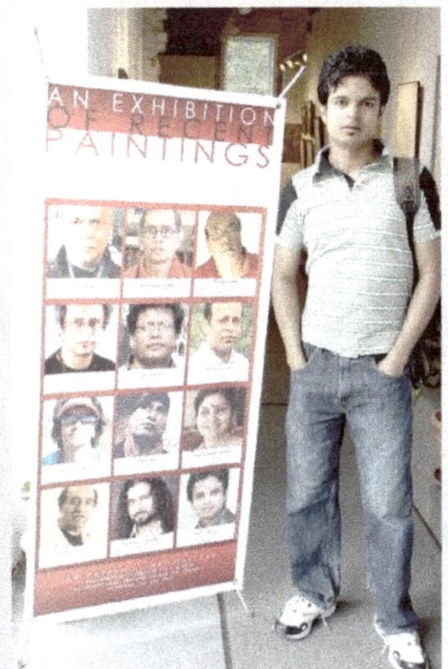

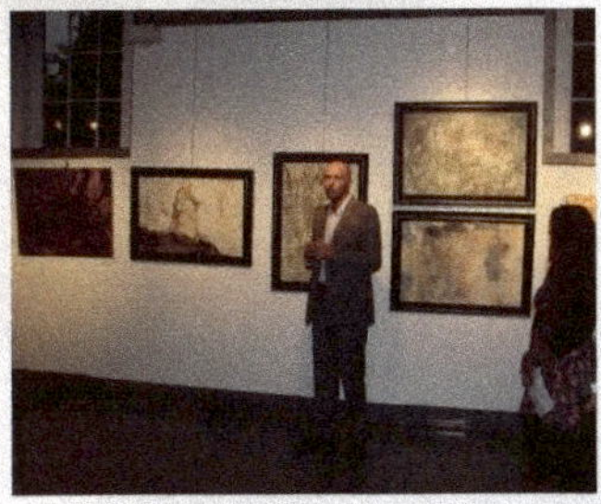

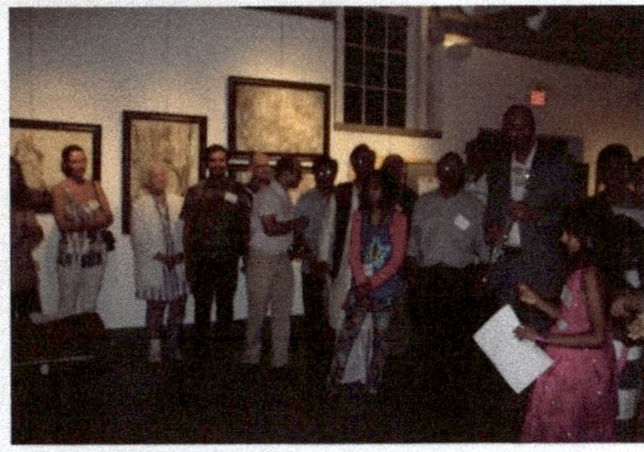

"contemporary painting exhibition, 2011" venue: papermill art gallery, Toronto, Canada, number of participants: 12, duration: 31st may-13th June.

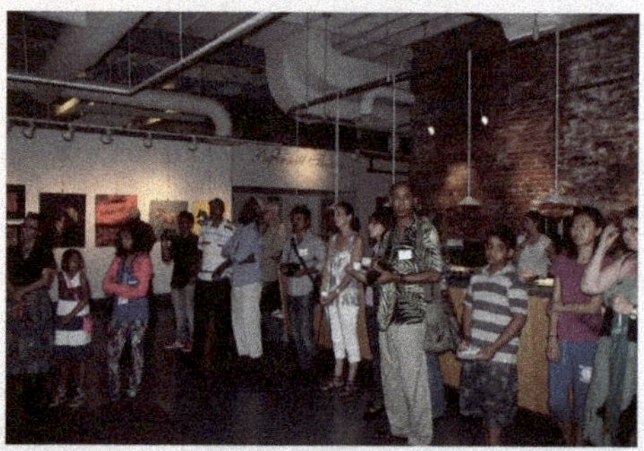

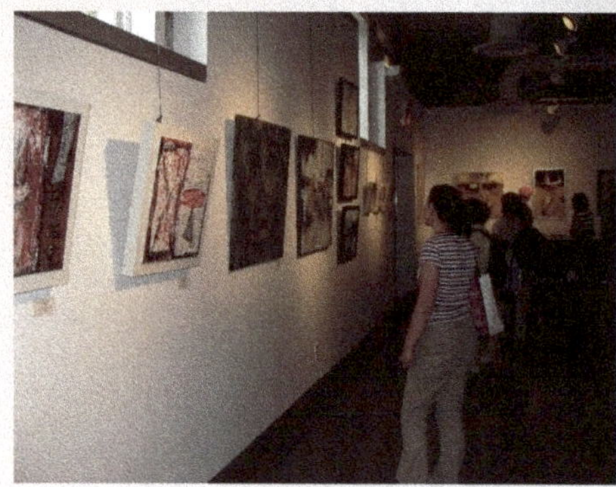

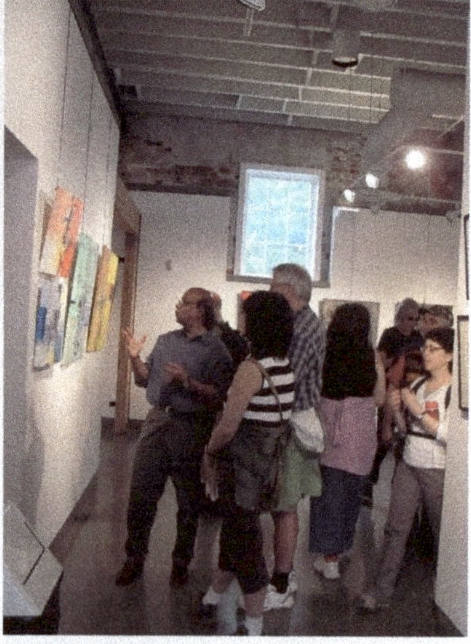

"contemporary painting exhibition, 2011" venue: papermill
art gallery, Toronto, Canada, number of participants: 12,
duration: 31st may-13th June.

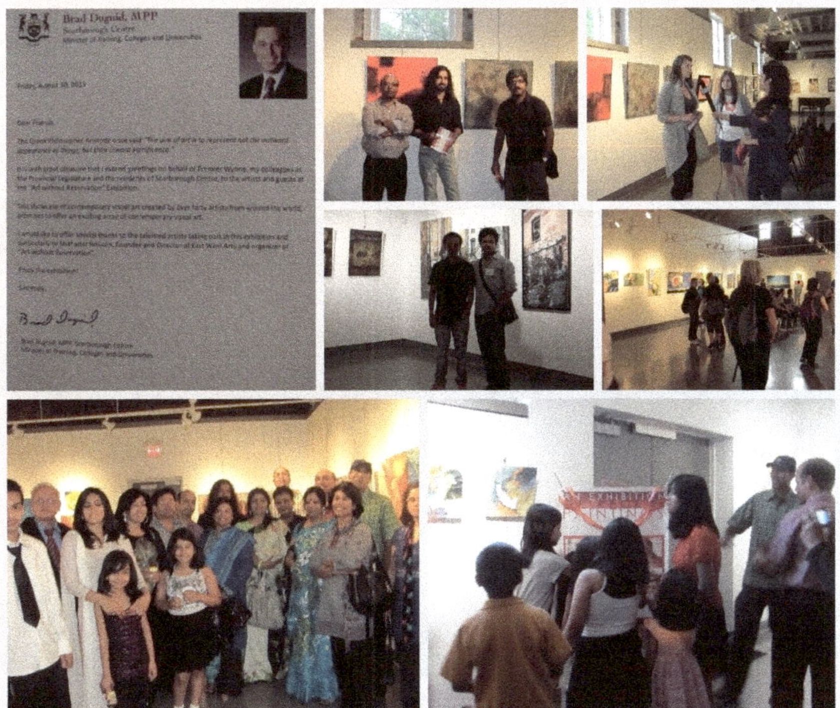

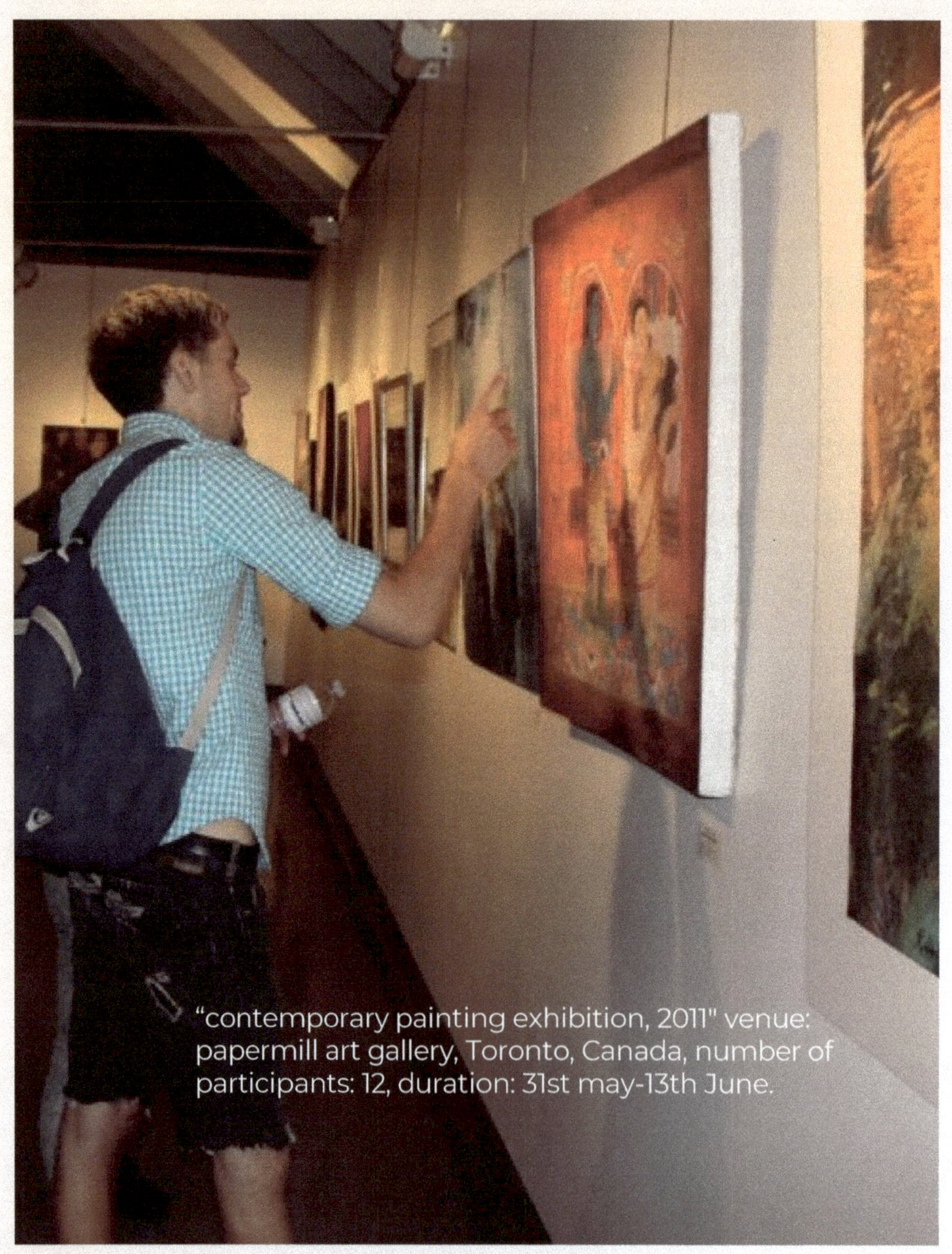

"contemporary painting exhibition, 2011" venue: papermill art gallery, Toronto, Canada, number of participants: 12, duration: 31st may-13th June.

EXOTIC ARTWORKS

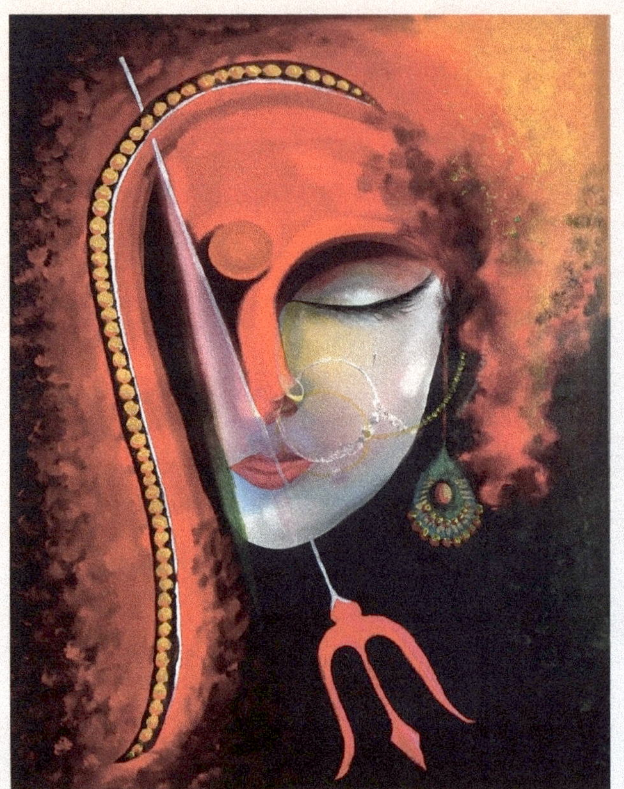

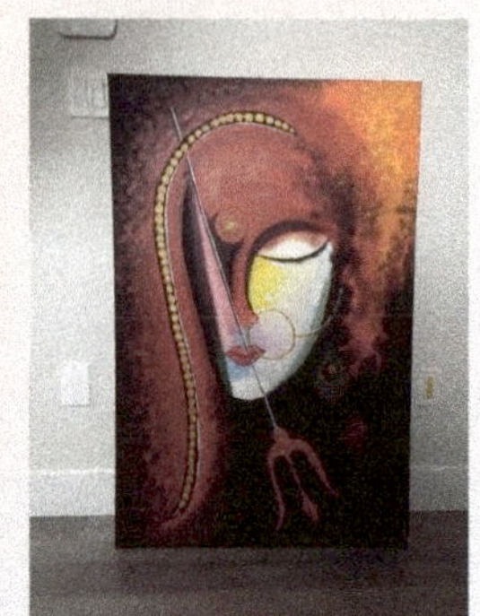

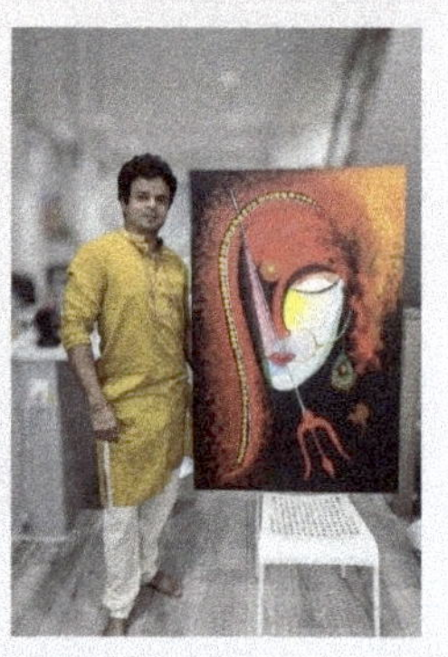

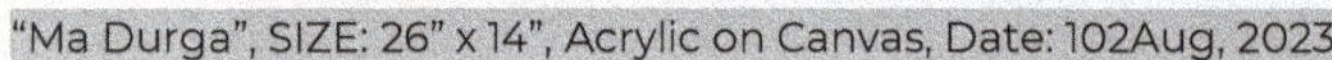

"Ma Durga", SIZE: 26" x 14", Acrylic on Canvas, Date: 102Aug, 2023

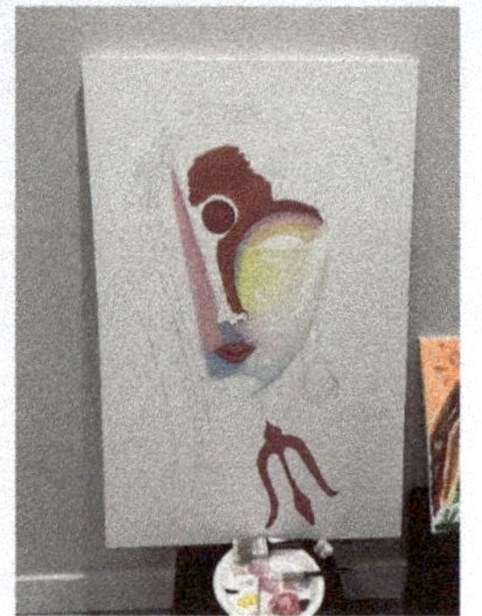

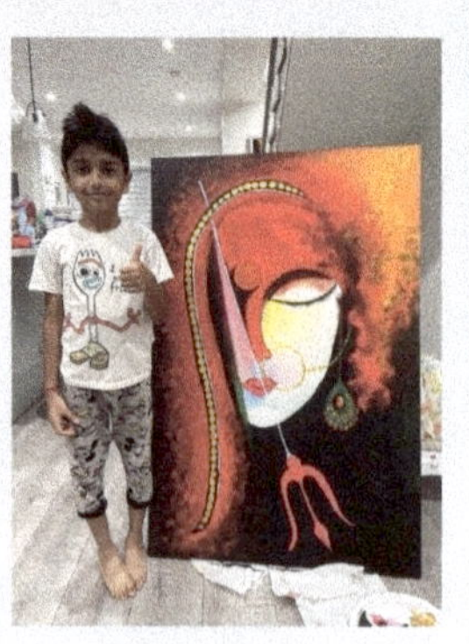

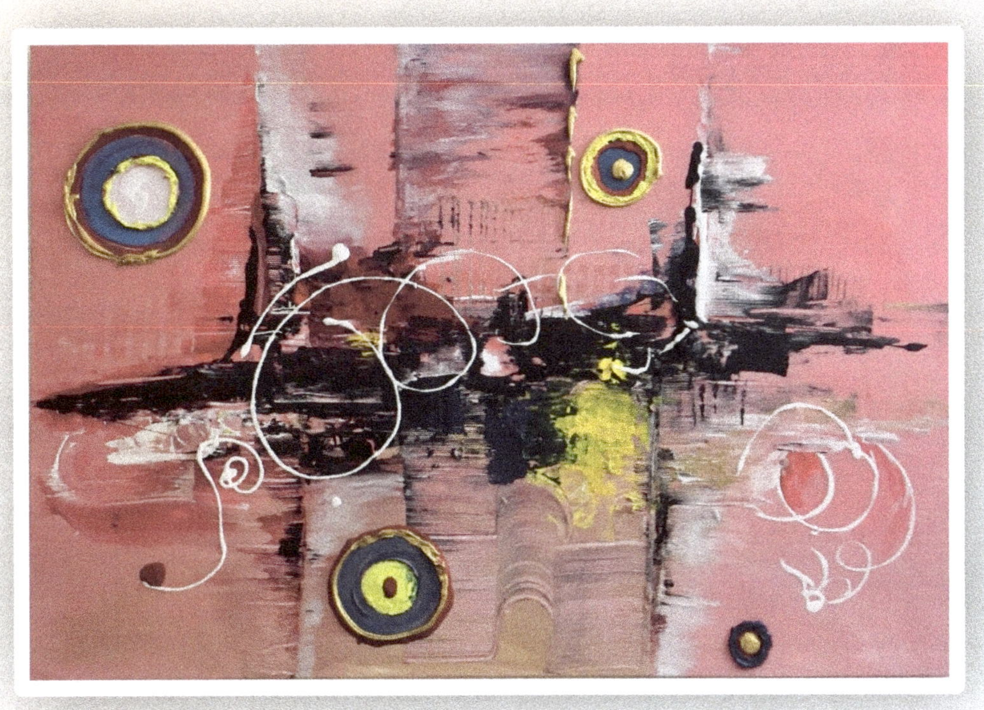

"NOYONTARA", SIZE: 26" x 14", Acrylic on Canvas, Date: 10 Aug, 2020

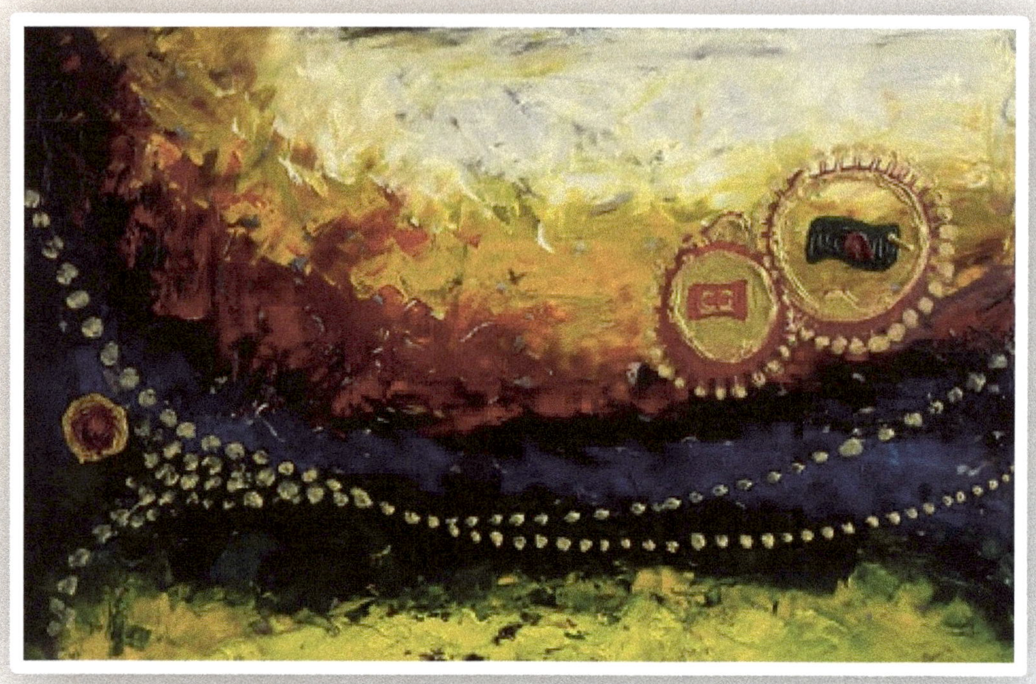

"COVID RACE", SIZE: 40" x 26", Acrylic on Canvas, Date: 10 Aug, 2020

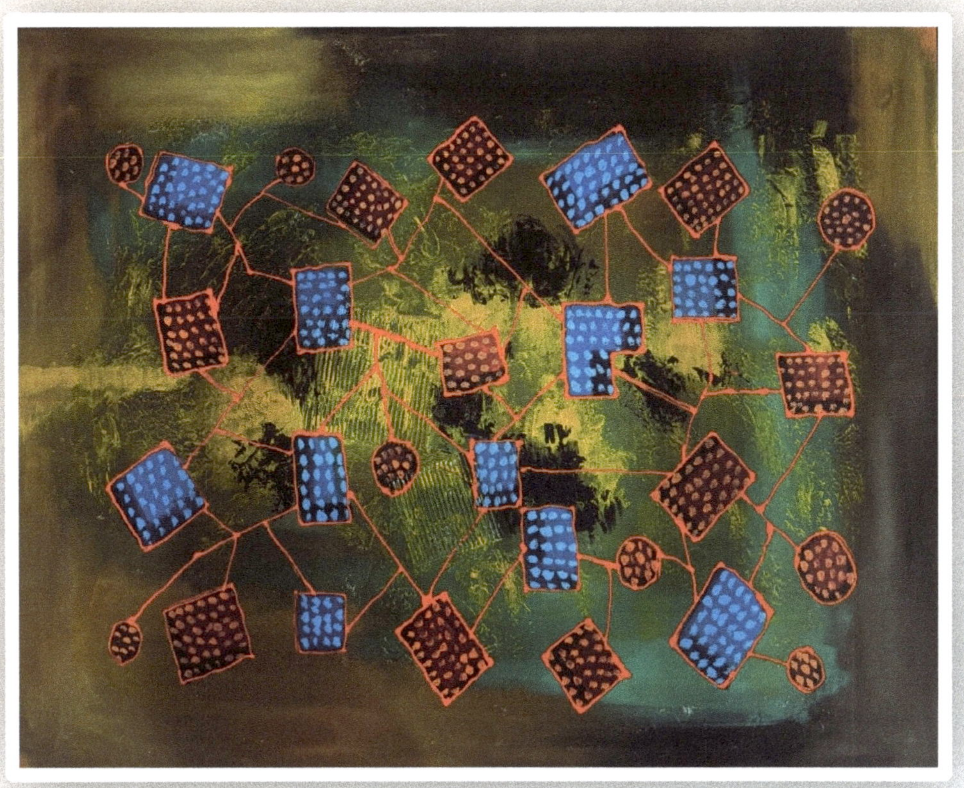

"AI Network", SIZE: 40" x 26", Acrylic on Canvas, Date: 12 Feb, 2024

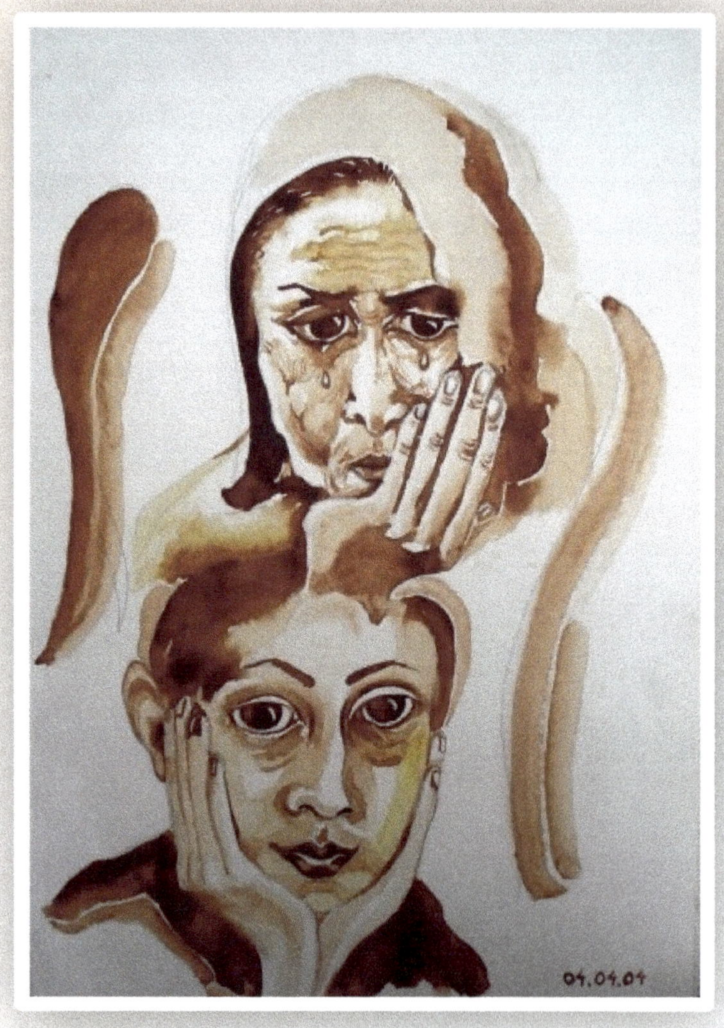

Age difference
16 H X 10 W inch
Water color on paper
Nov 2008

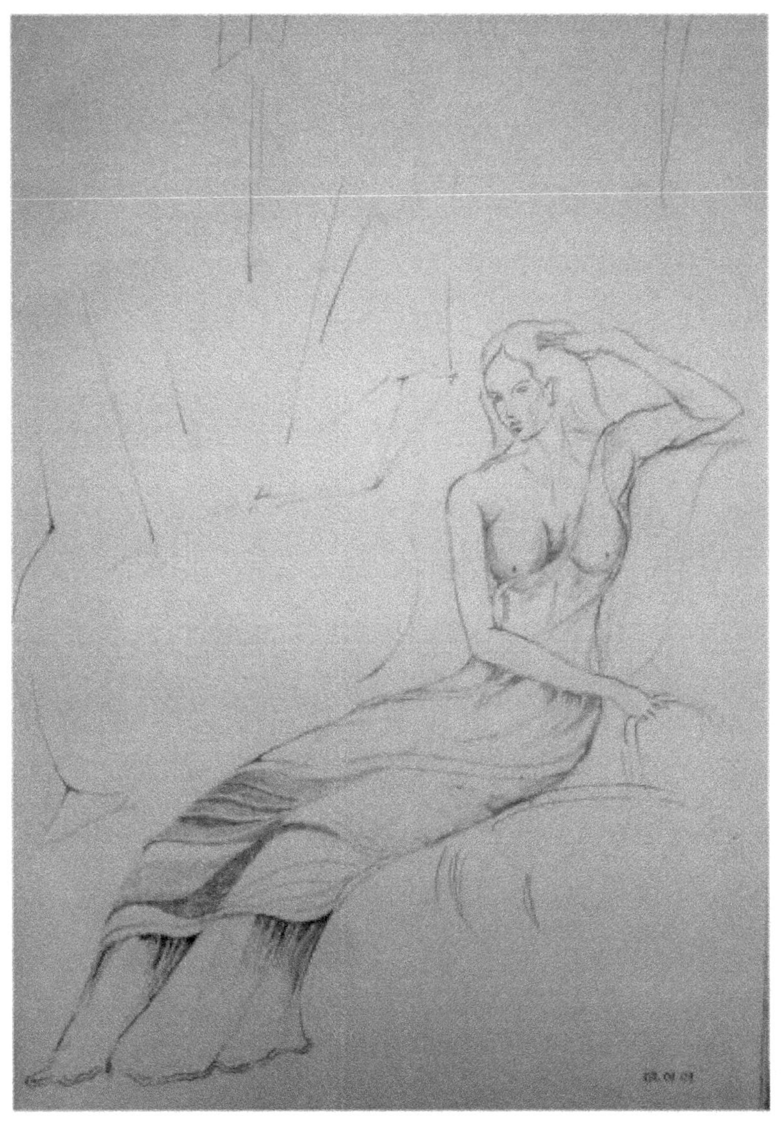

"Drawing study"

Pencil sketch on paper

Size: 18 X 24 inch,

Date: August, 2010,

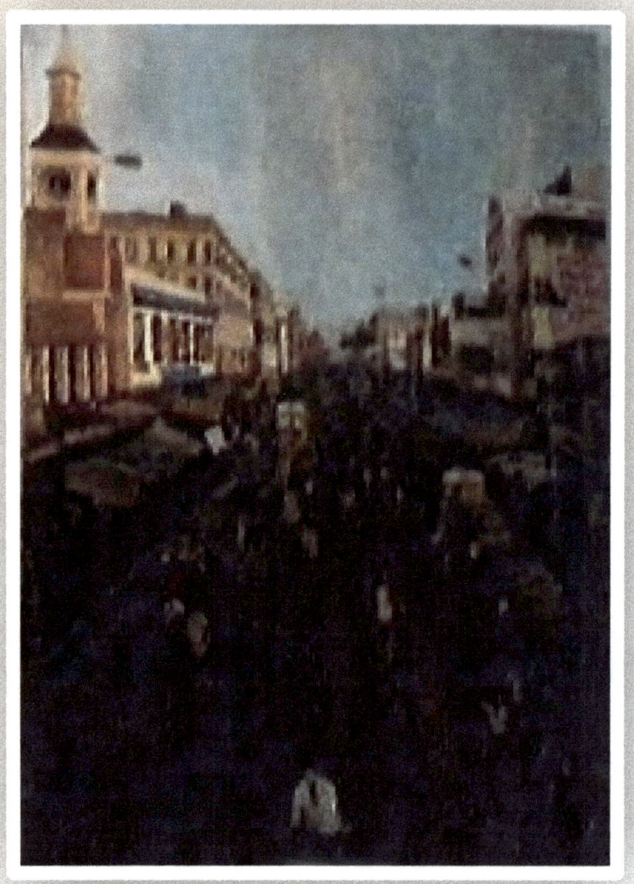

Old Dhaka
18 H X 36 W inches
Oil paint on canvas
Jan 2010

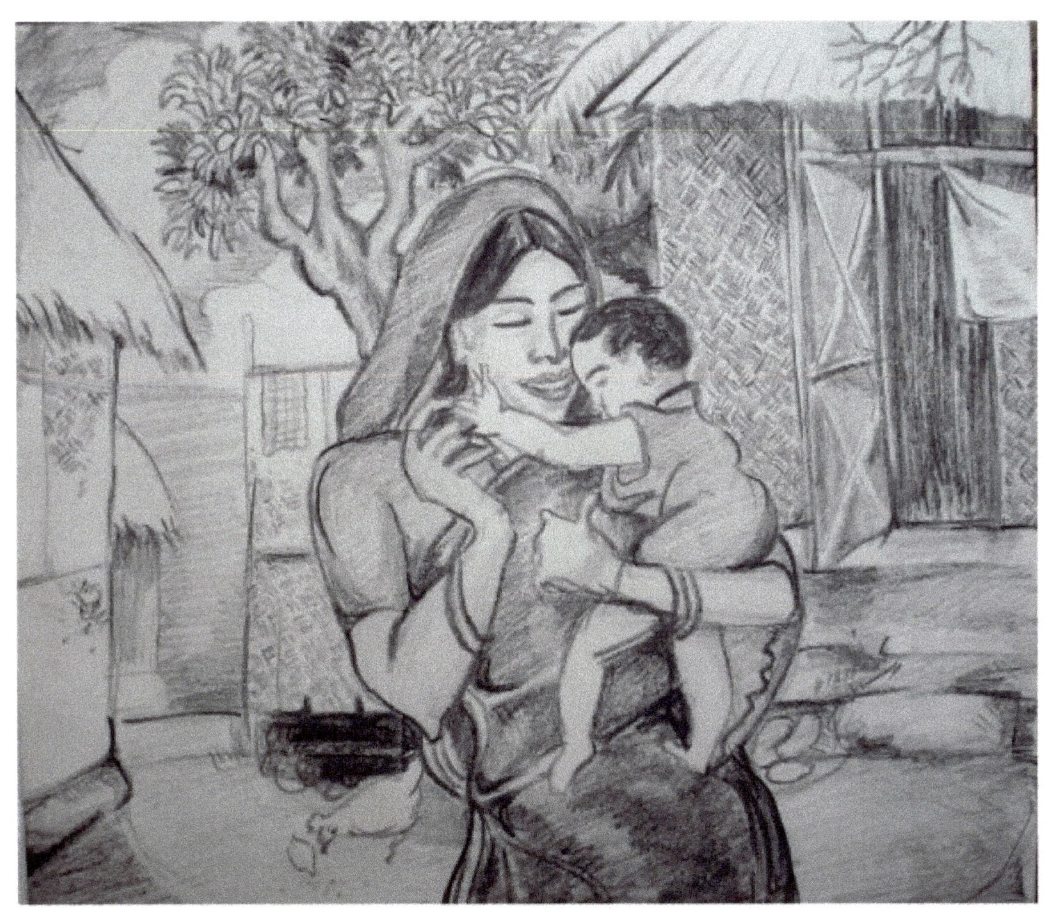

"A mother and son"

Pencil sketch on paper

Size: 18 X 24 inch,

Date: August, 2010,

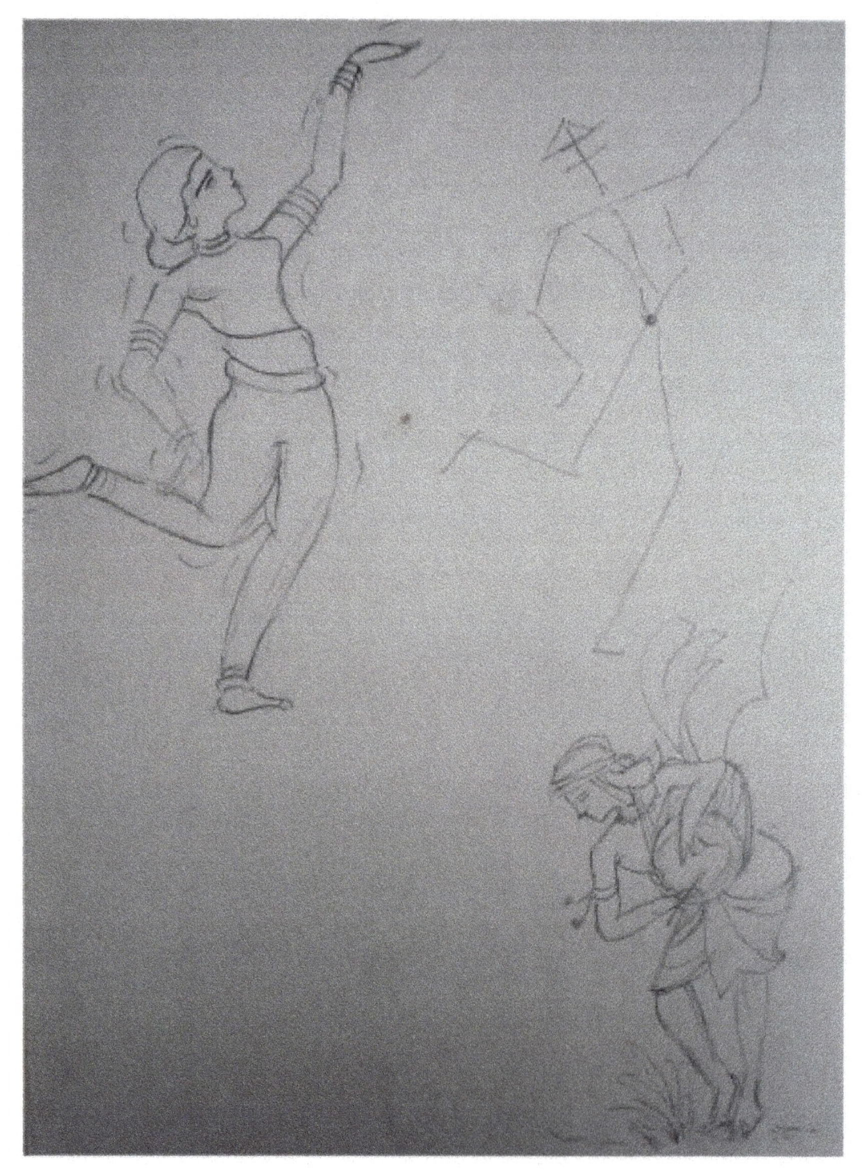

"Drawing study"

Pencil sketch on paper

Size: 18 X 24 inch,

Date: August, 2010,

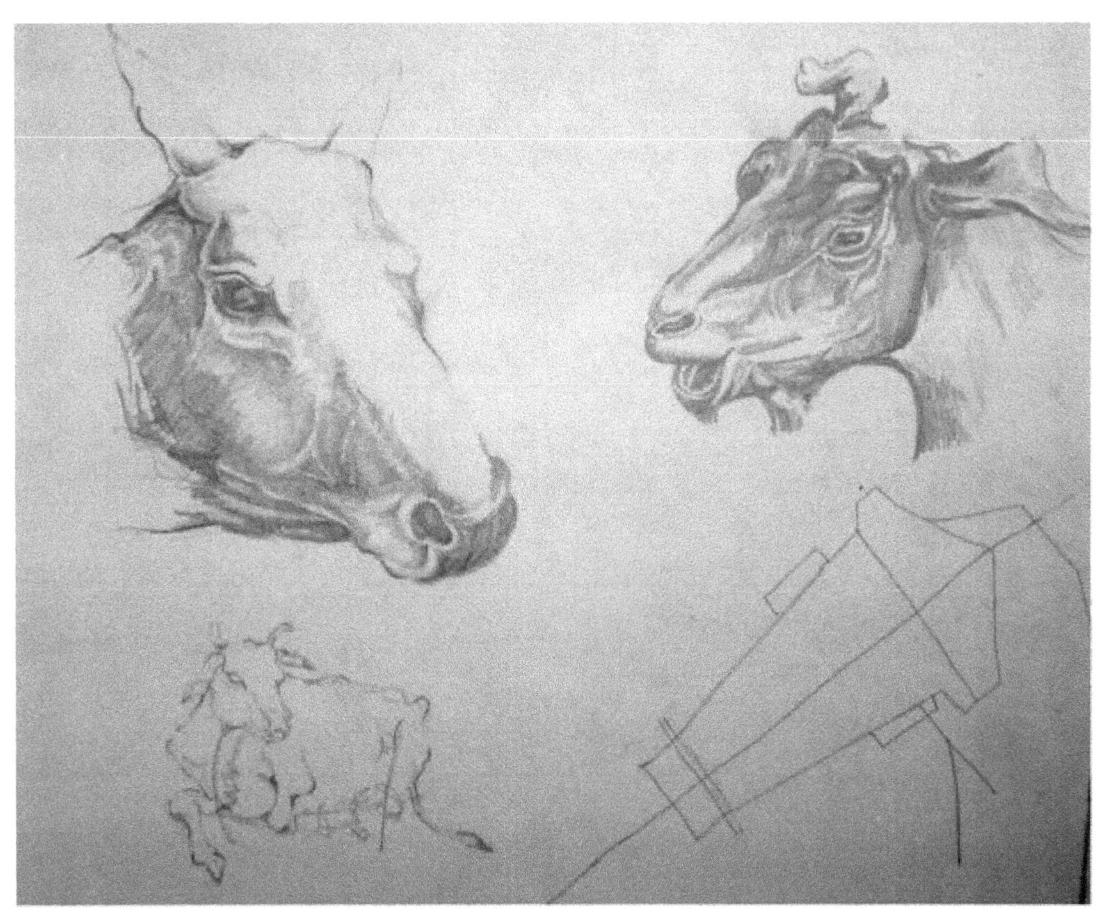

"Drawing study"

Pencil sketch on paper

Size: 18 X 24 inch,

Date: August, 2010,

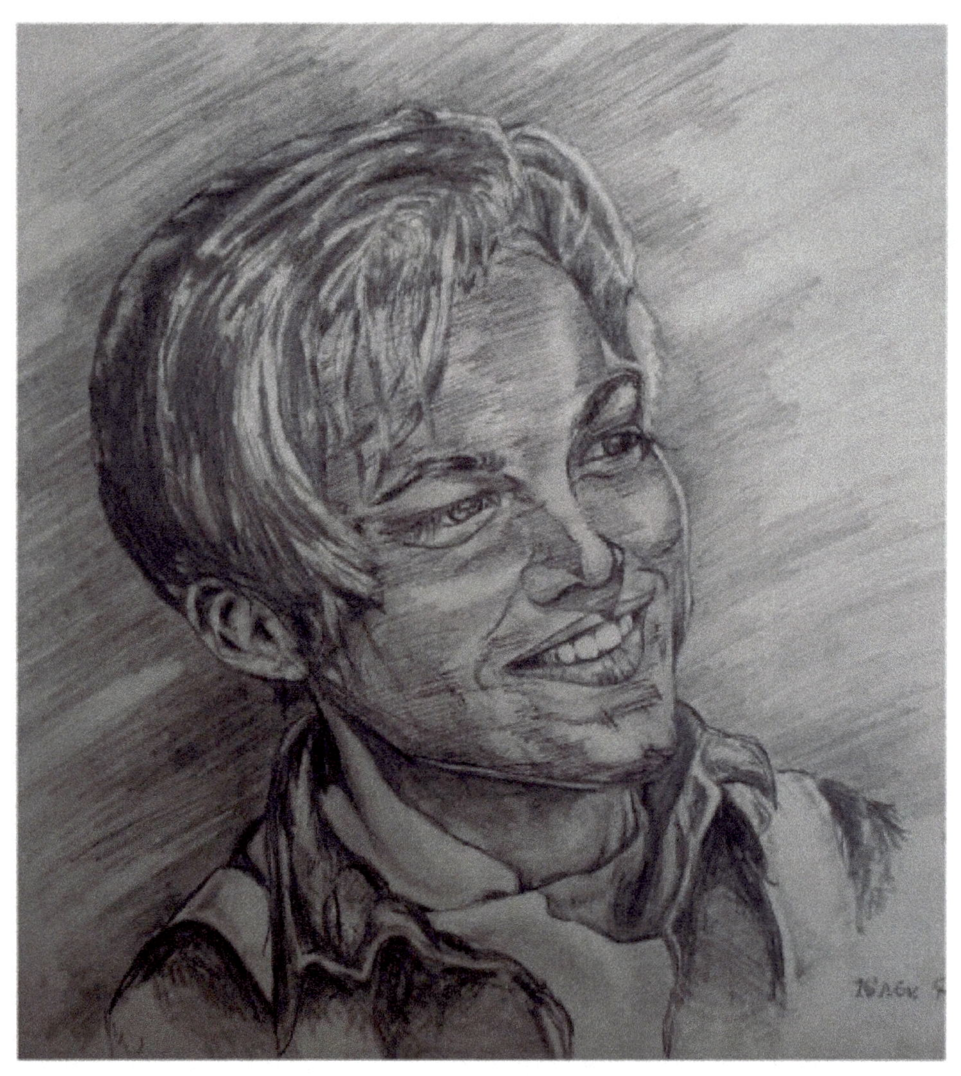

"Leonardo De Caprio"

Pencil sketch on paper

Size: 18 X 24 inch,

Date: July, 2011,

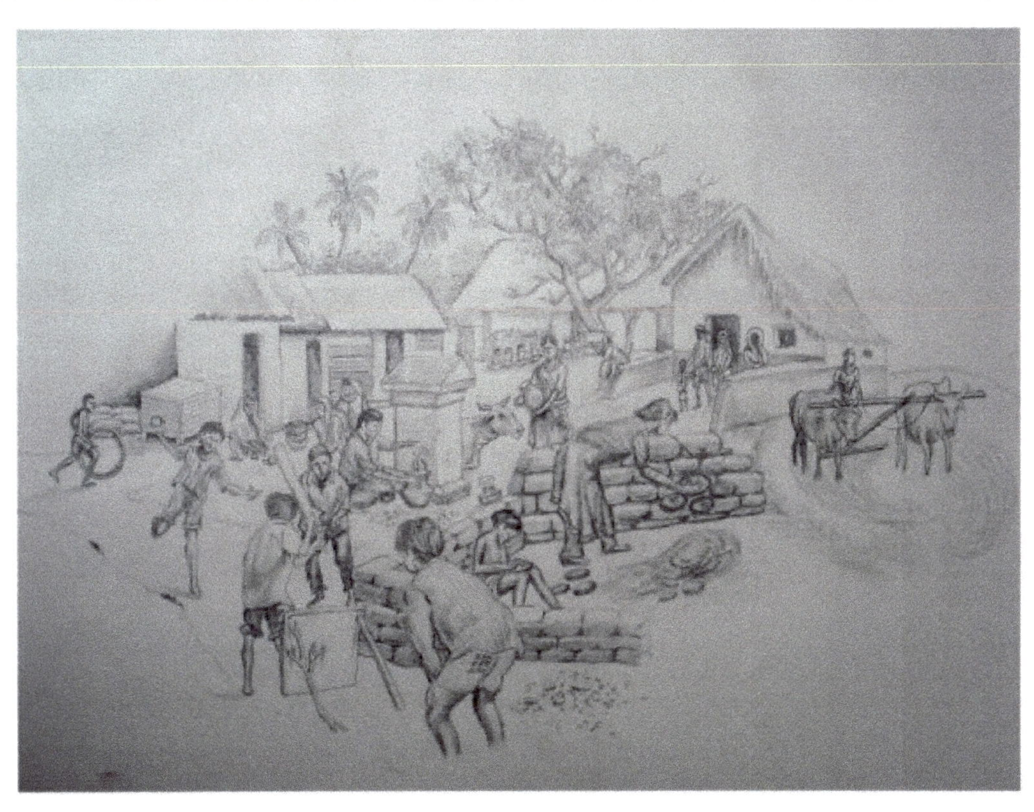

"Rural lifestyle"

Pencil sketch on paper

Size: 18 X 24 inch,

Date: May, 2002,

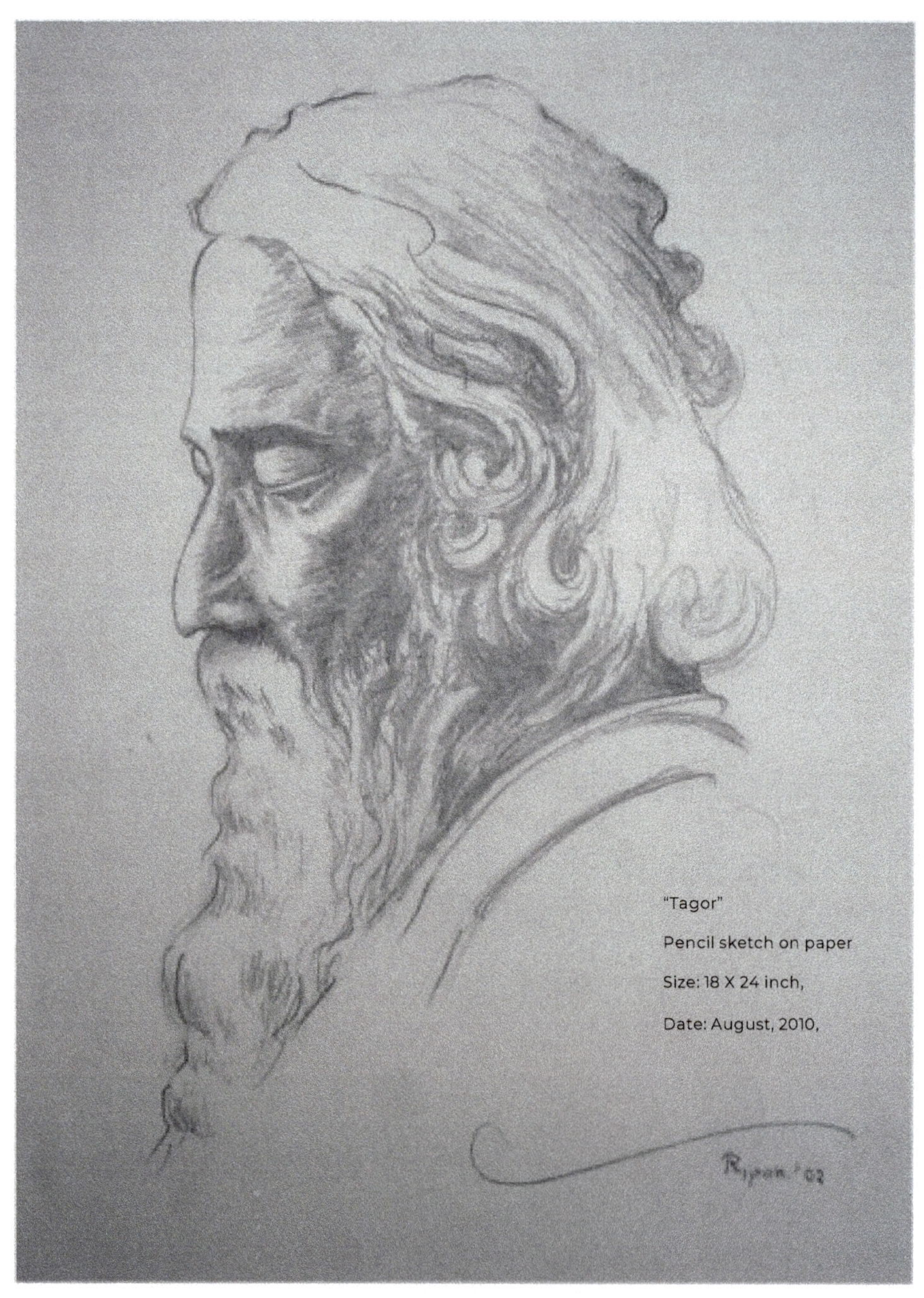

"Tagor"
Pencil sketch on paper
Size: 18 X 24 inch,
Date: August, 2010,

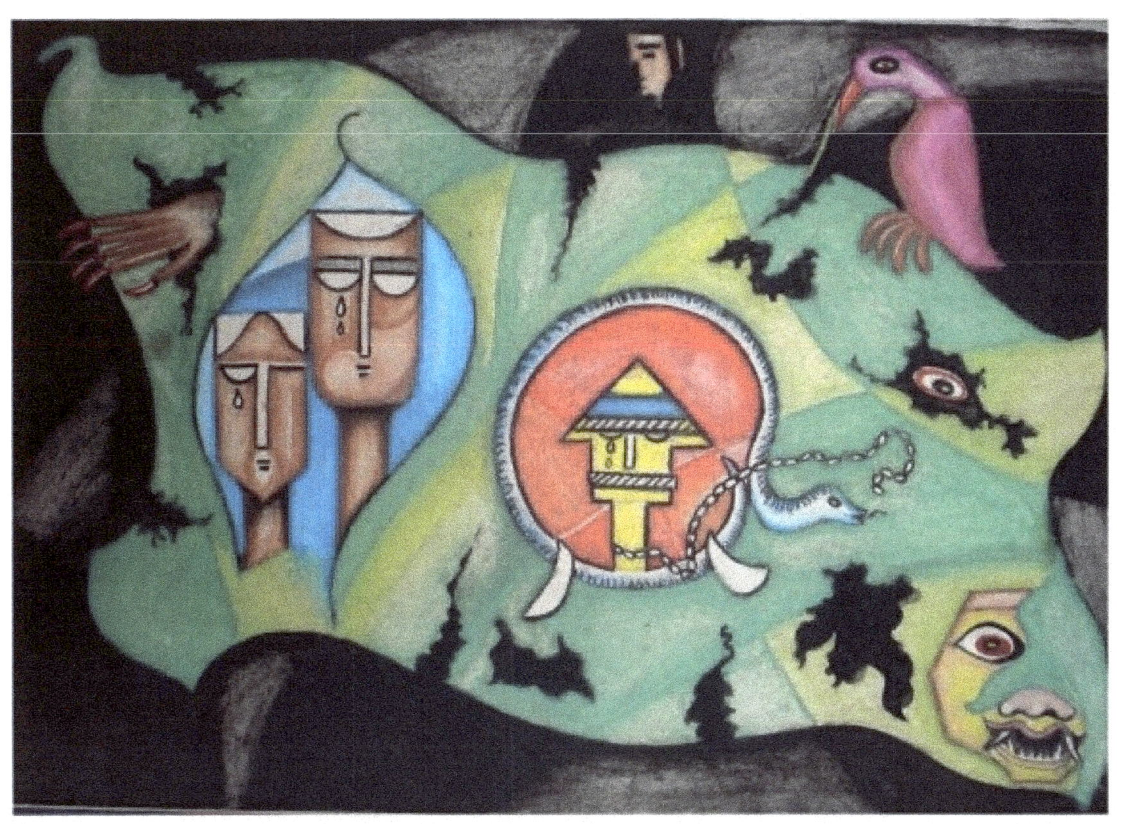

Dishonour to Flag
16 H X 10 W inch
Mixed media on paper
Nov 2008

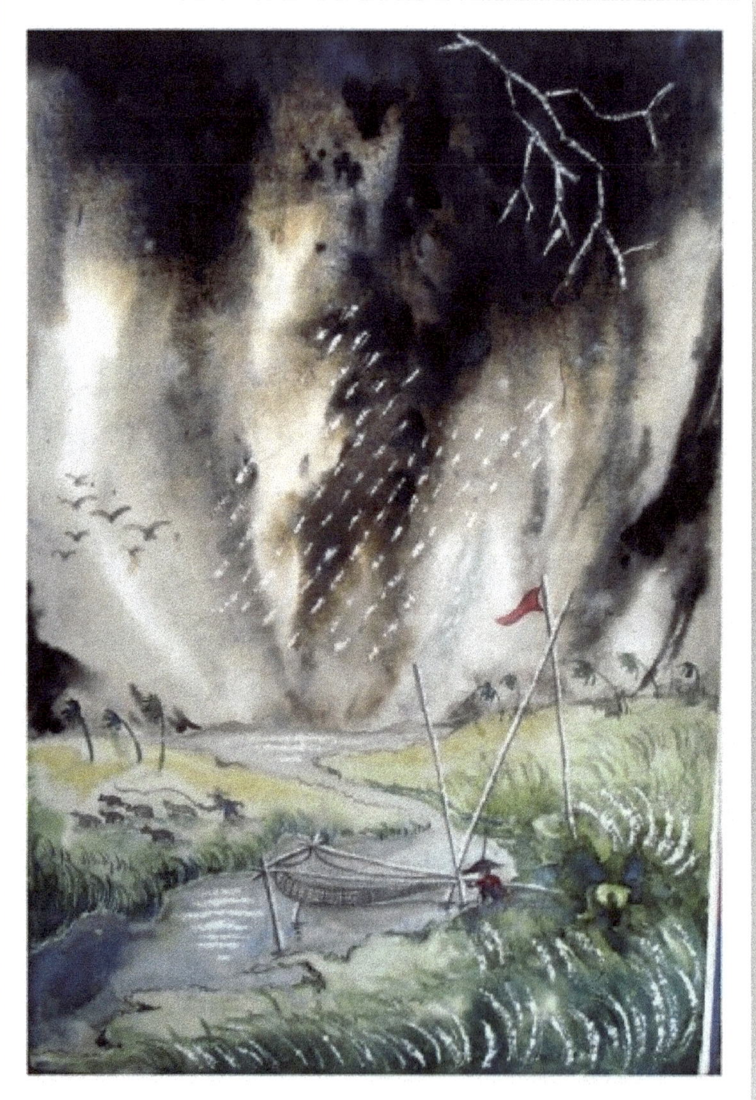

Feel the Cloud
16 H X 10 W inch
Mix media on paper
July 2007

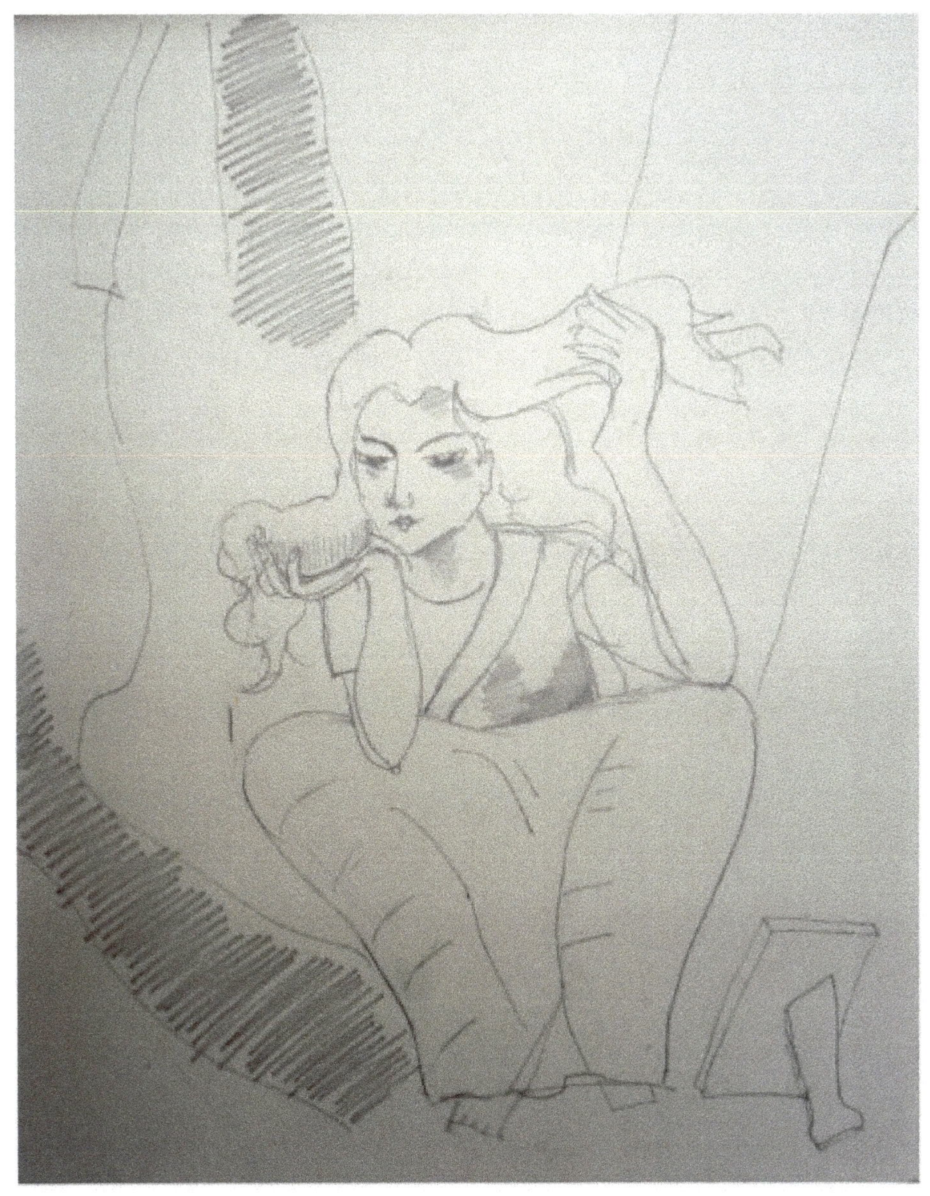

"Village girl"

Pencil sketch on paper

Size: 18 X 24 inch,

Date: August, 2010,

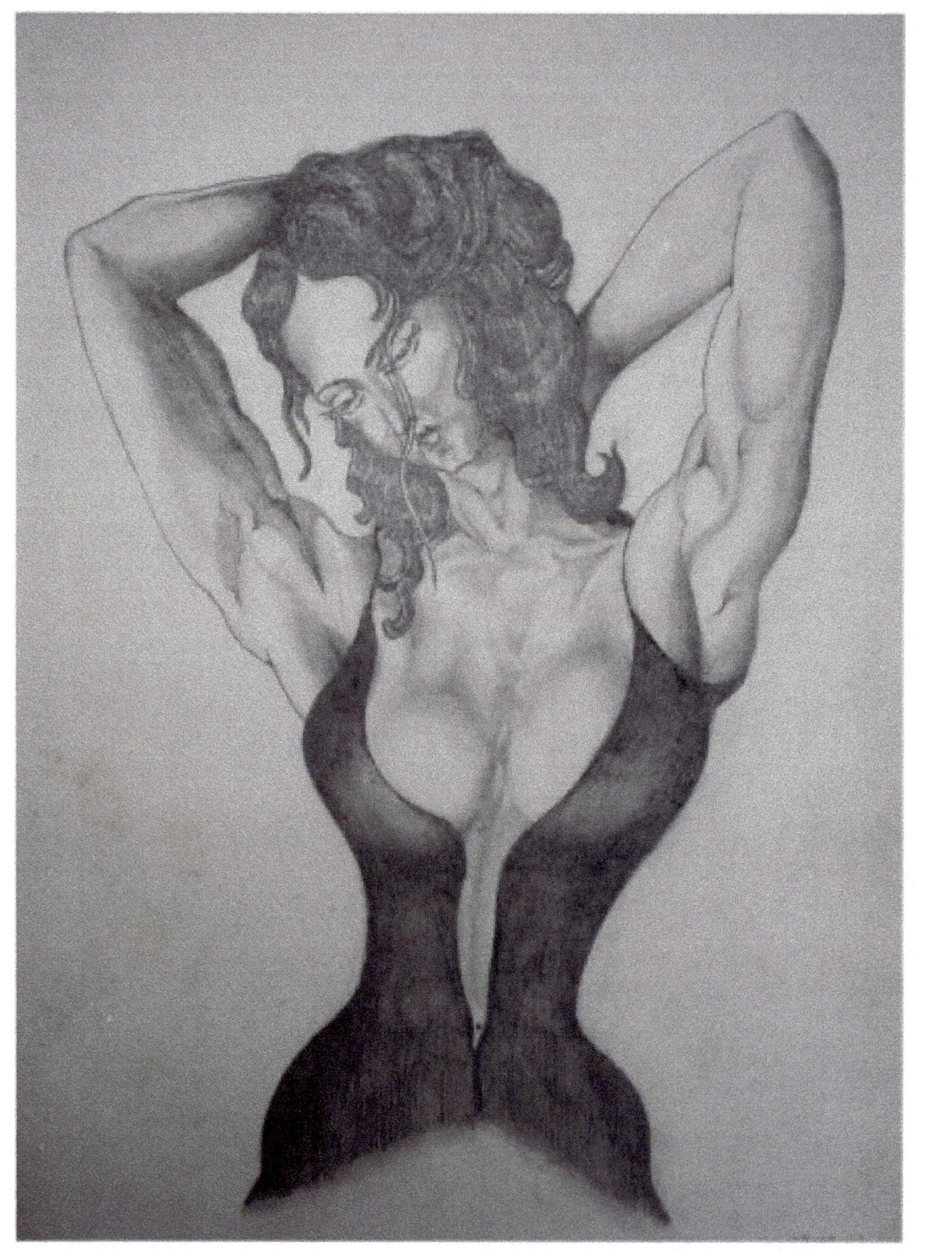

"A Girl"

Pencil sketch on paper

Size: 18 X 24 inch,

Date: August, 2010,

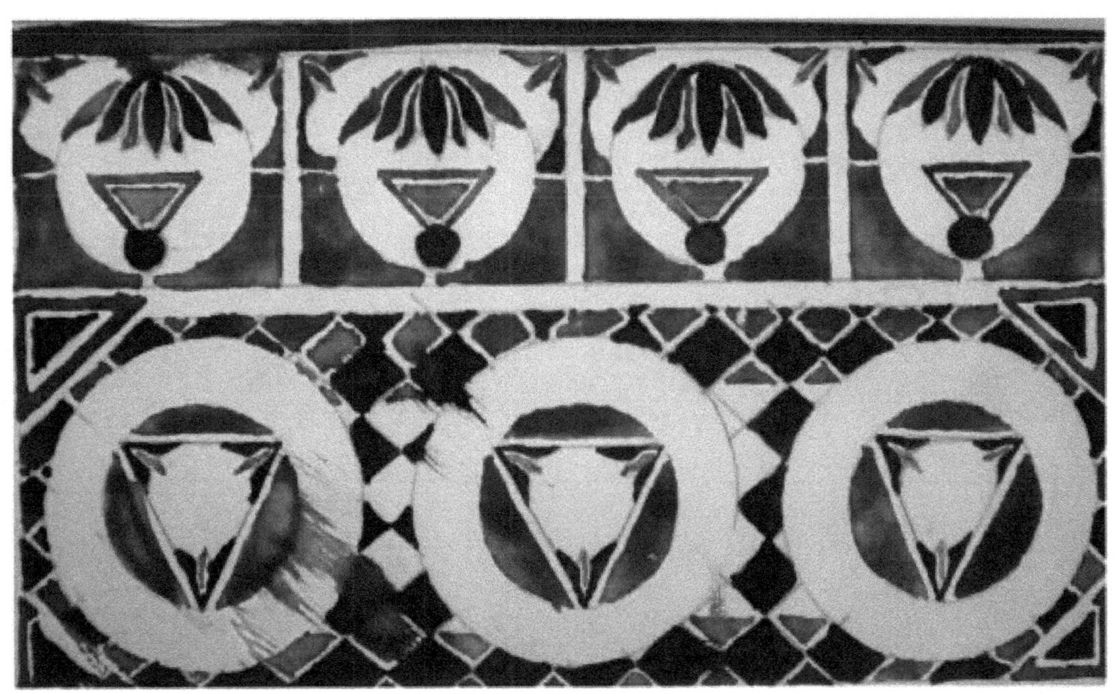

"Chapchitro"

Pain on paper

Size: 18 X 24 inch,

Date: June, 2006,

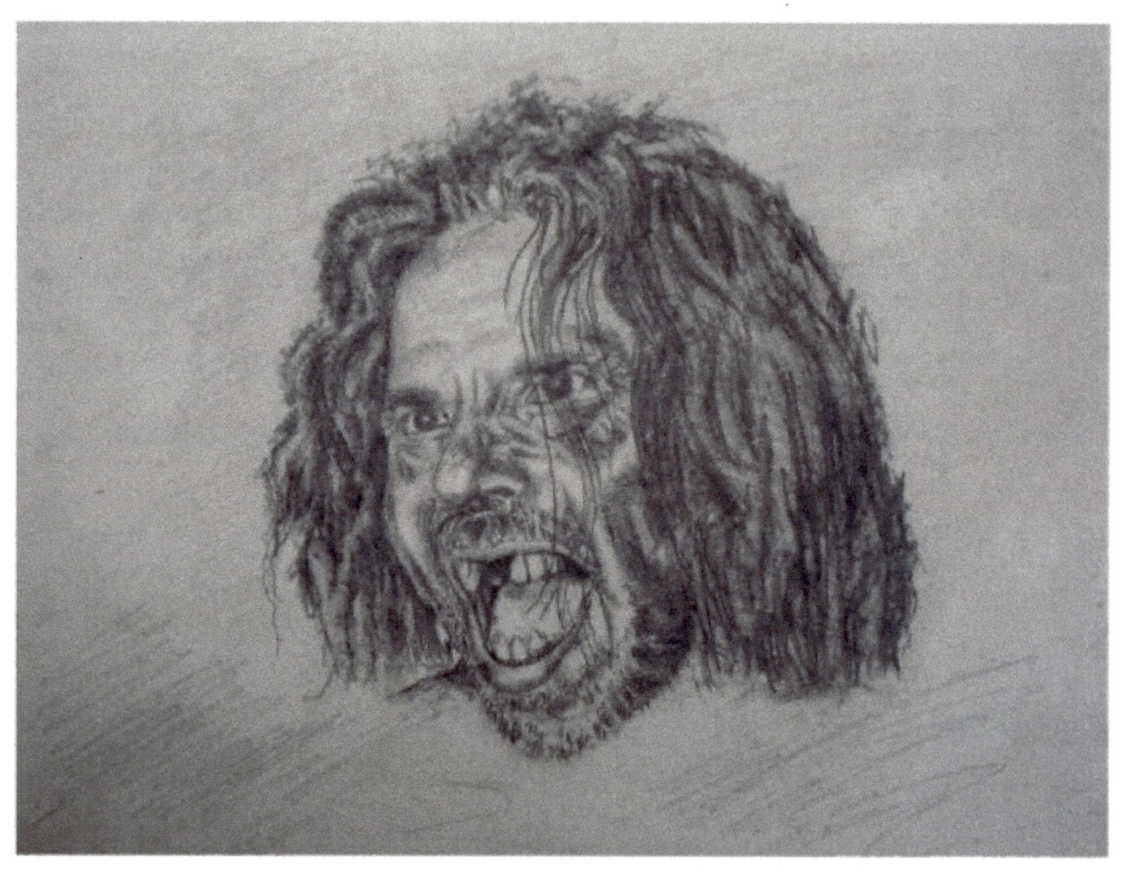

"Devil"

Pencil sketch on paper

Size: 18 X 24 inch,

Date: August, 2010,

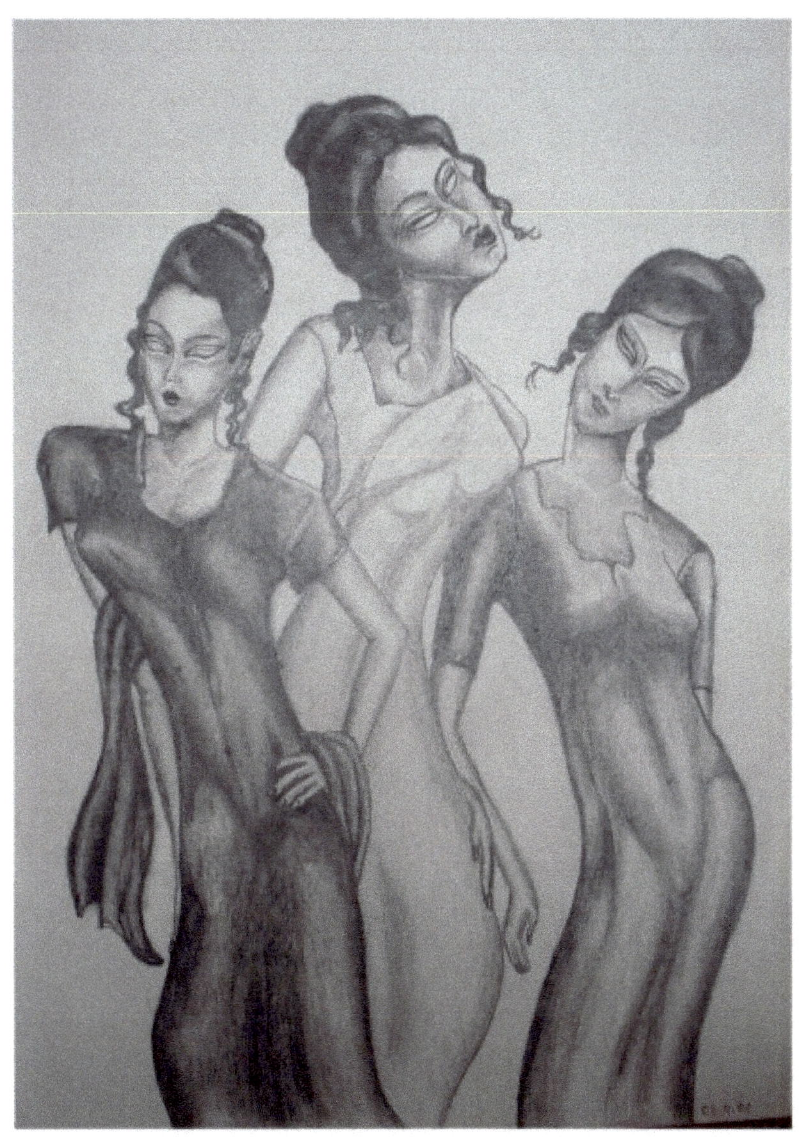

"Village girl"

Pencil sketch on paper

Size: 18 X 24 inch,

Date: Jan, 2005,

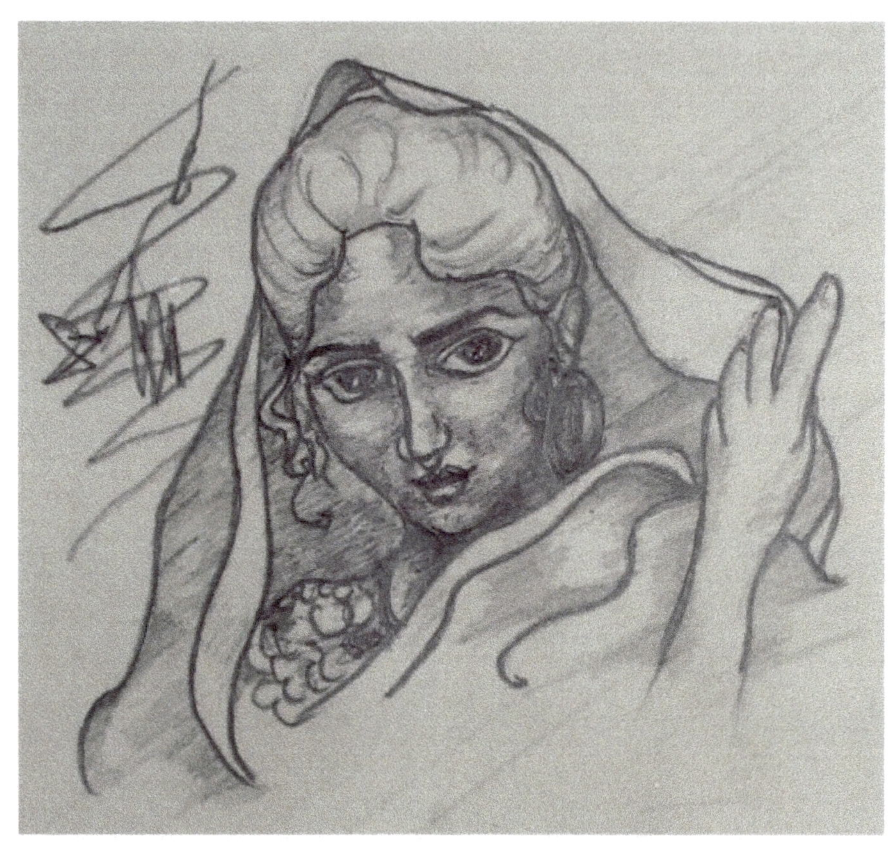

"Village girl"

Pencil sketch on paper

Size: 18 X 24 inch,

Date: August, 2010,

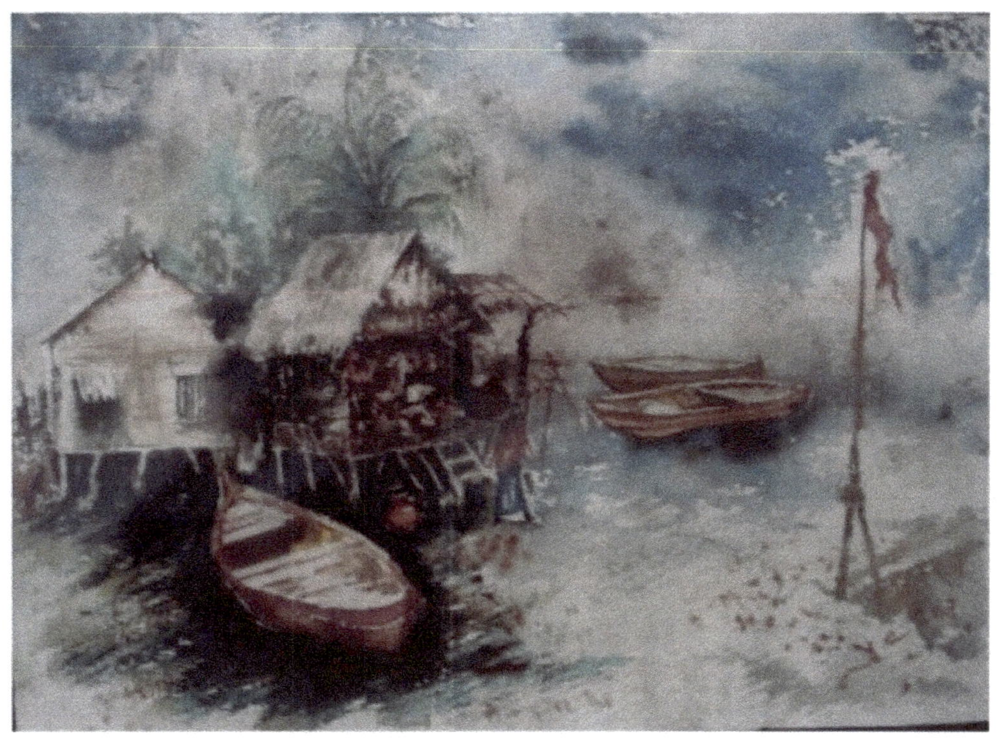

Waterfront
10 H X 16 W inches
Water color on paper
March 2007

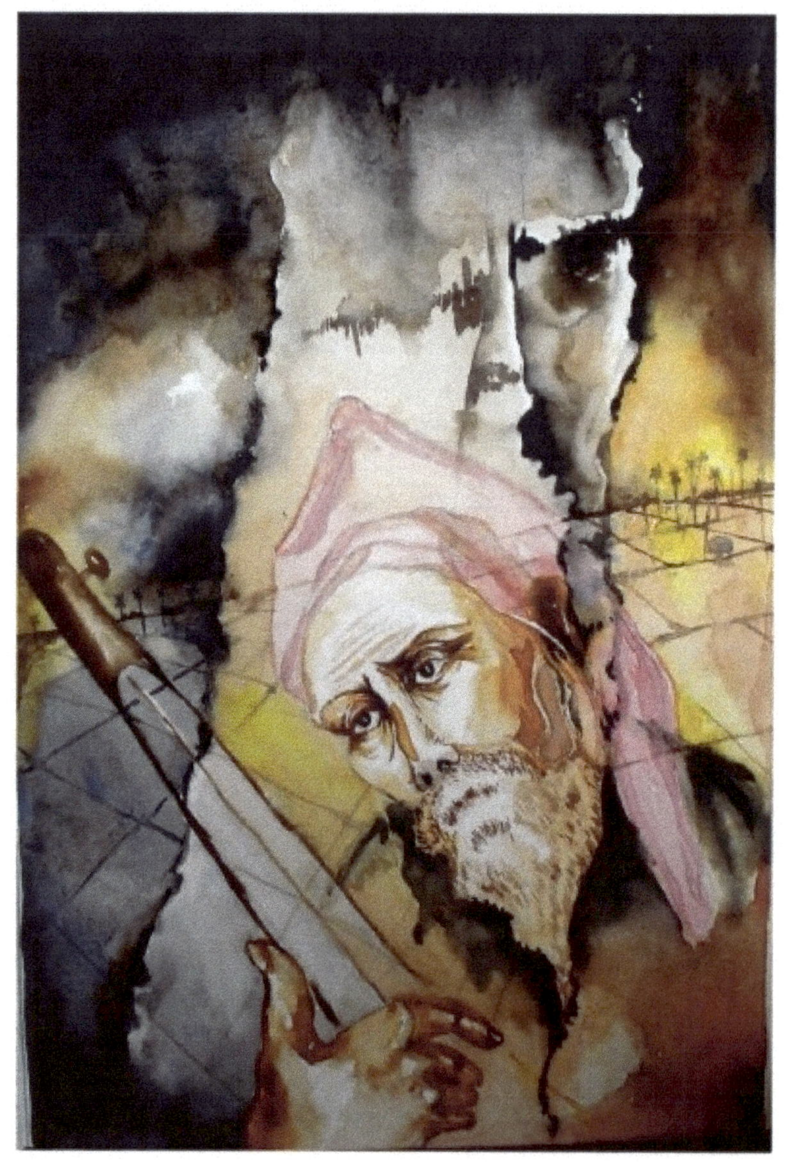

Baul
16 H X 10 W inches
Water color
March 2002

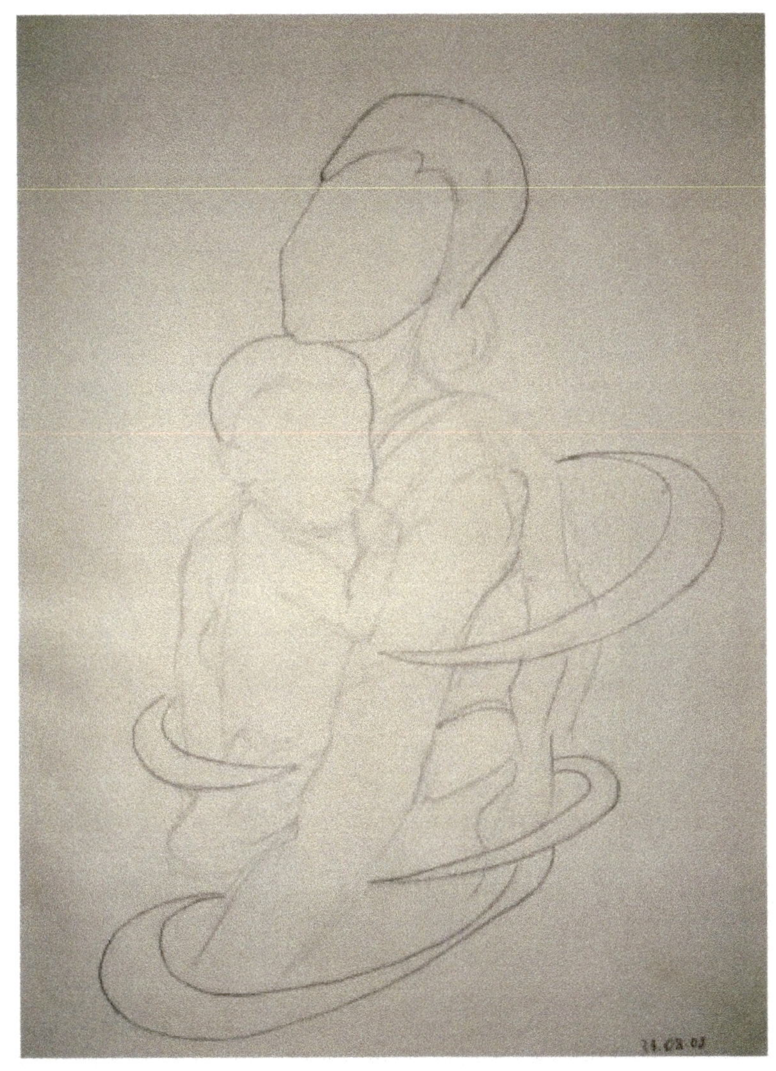

"Mother"

Pencil on paper

Size: 18 X 24 inch,

Date: August, 2013,

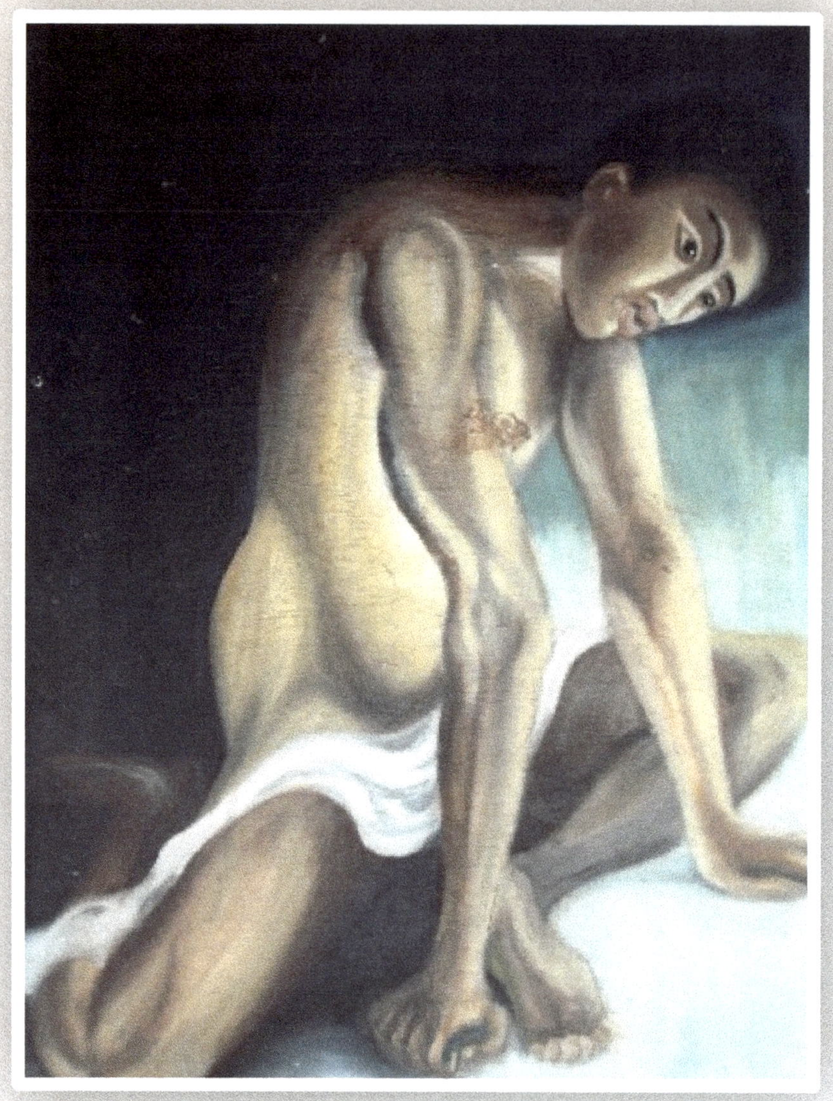

Adolescence
10 H X 16 W inch
Oil Painting
April, 2003

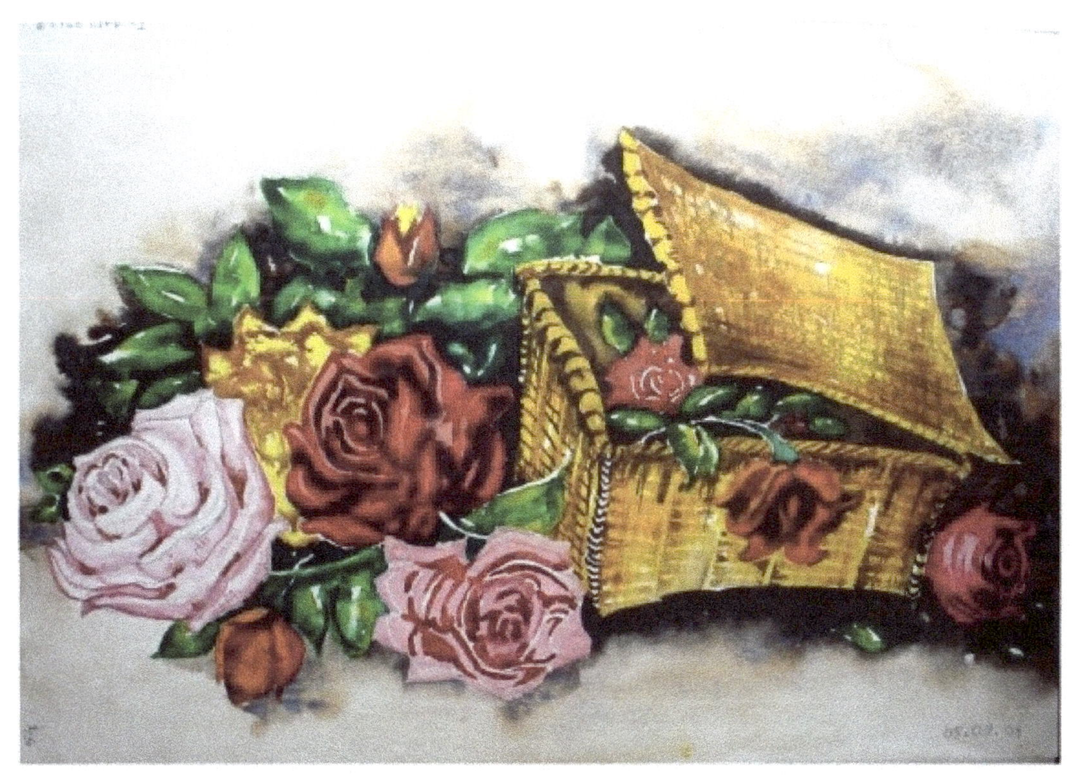

Flowers in bucket
16 H X 10 W inches
Water color on paper
Oct, 2010

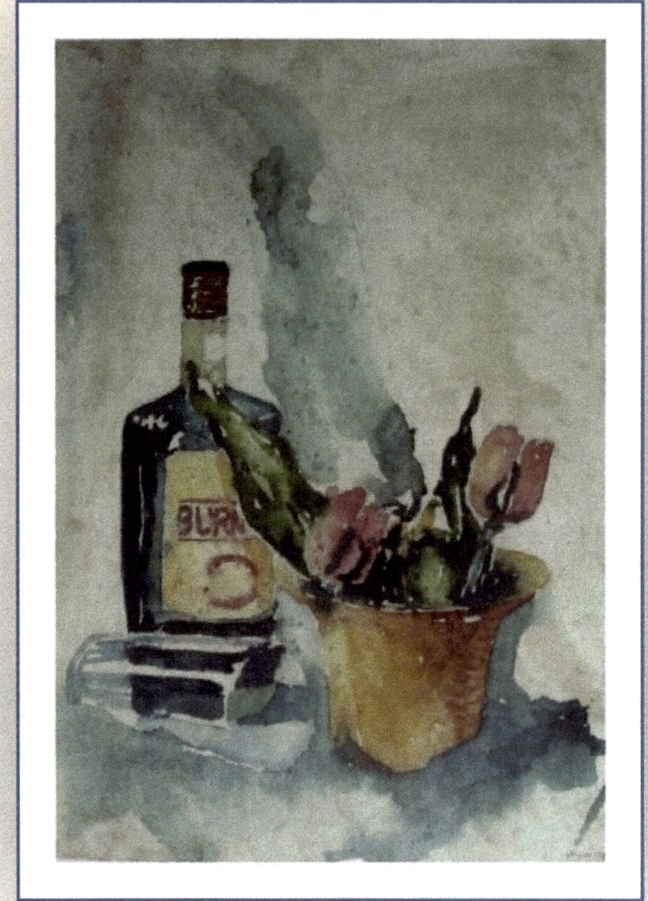

"Still life"
Water color on paper
Size: 18 X 24 inch,
Date: August, 2010,

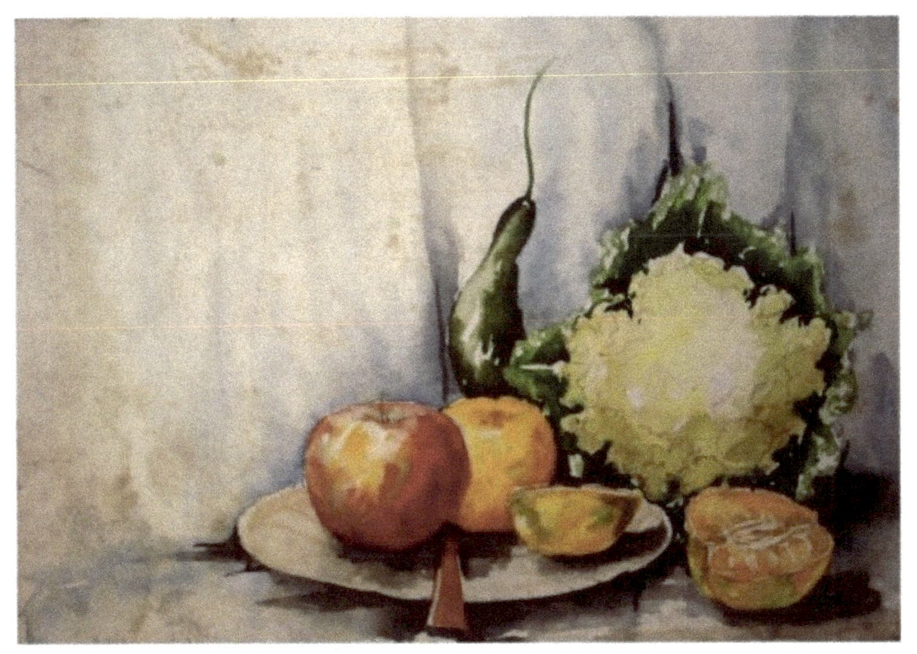

"Still life"

Water color on paper

Size: 18 X 24 inch,

Date: August, 2010,

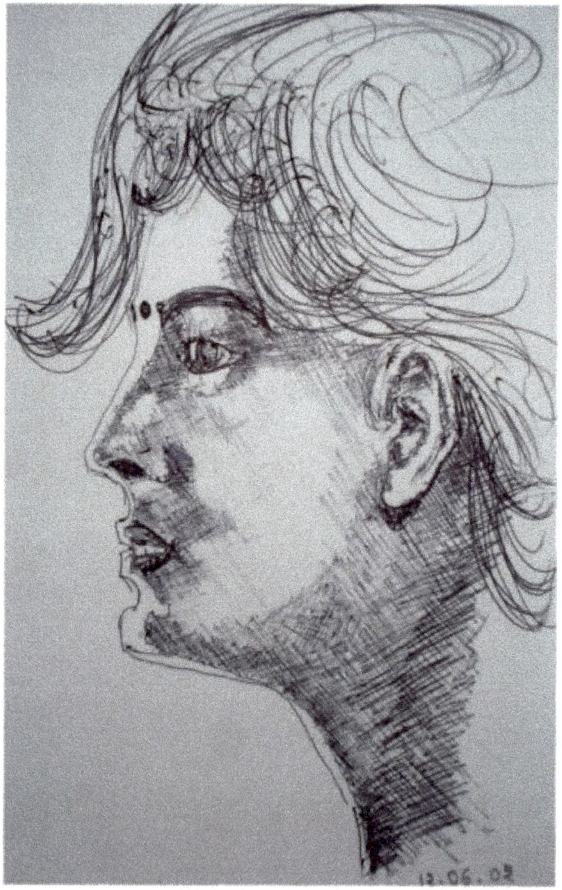

"A lady"

Pen on paper

Size: 18 X 24 inch,

Date: August, 2010,

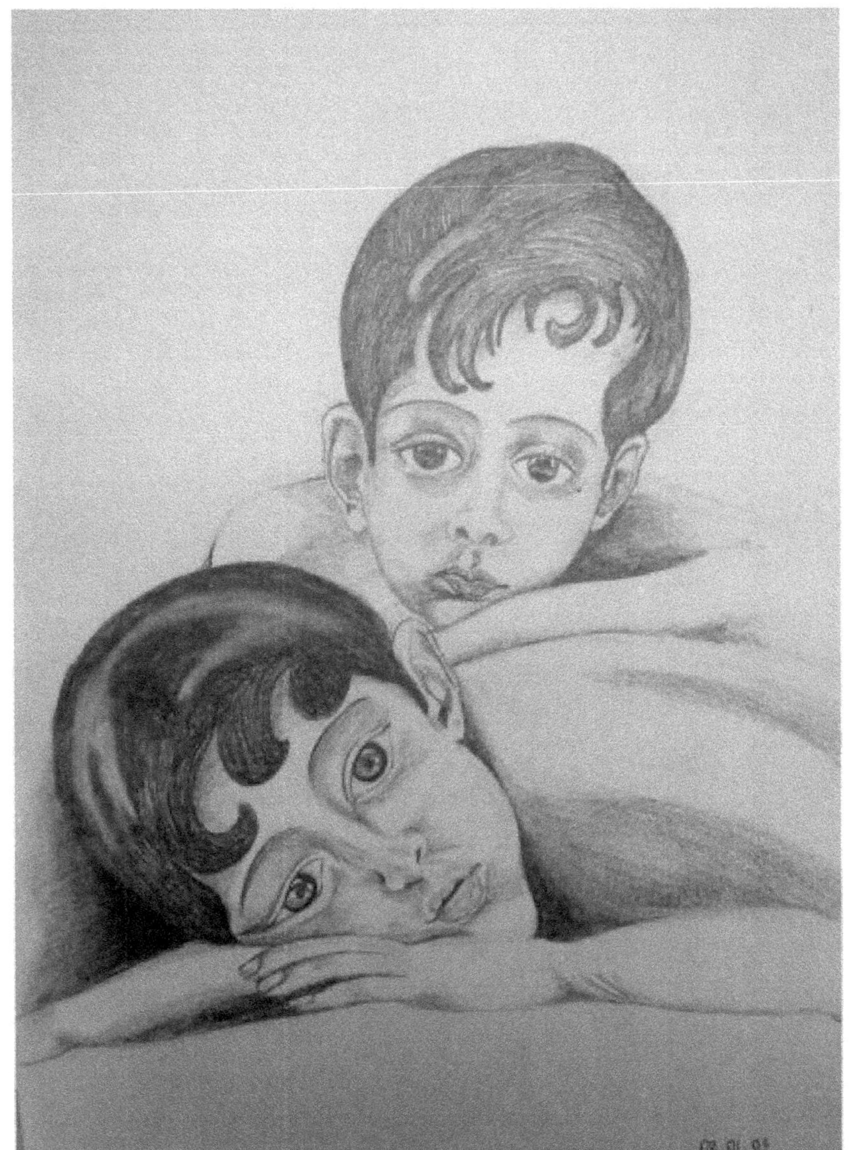

"Twin"

Pencil on paper

Size: 18 X 24 inch,

Date: August, 2010,

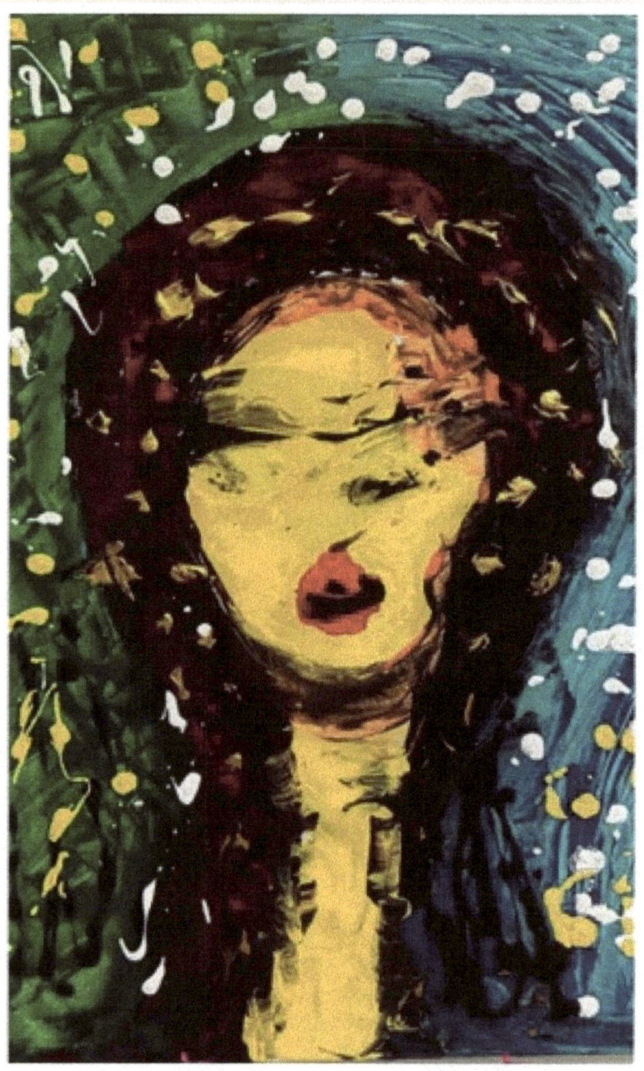

A Lady
16 H X 10 W inches
Acrylic on canvas
Feb 2008

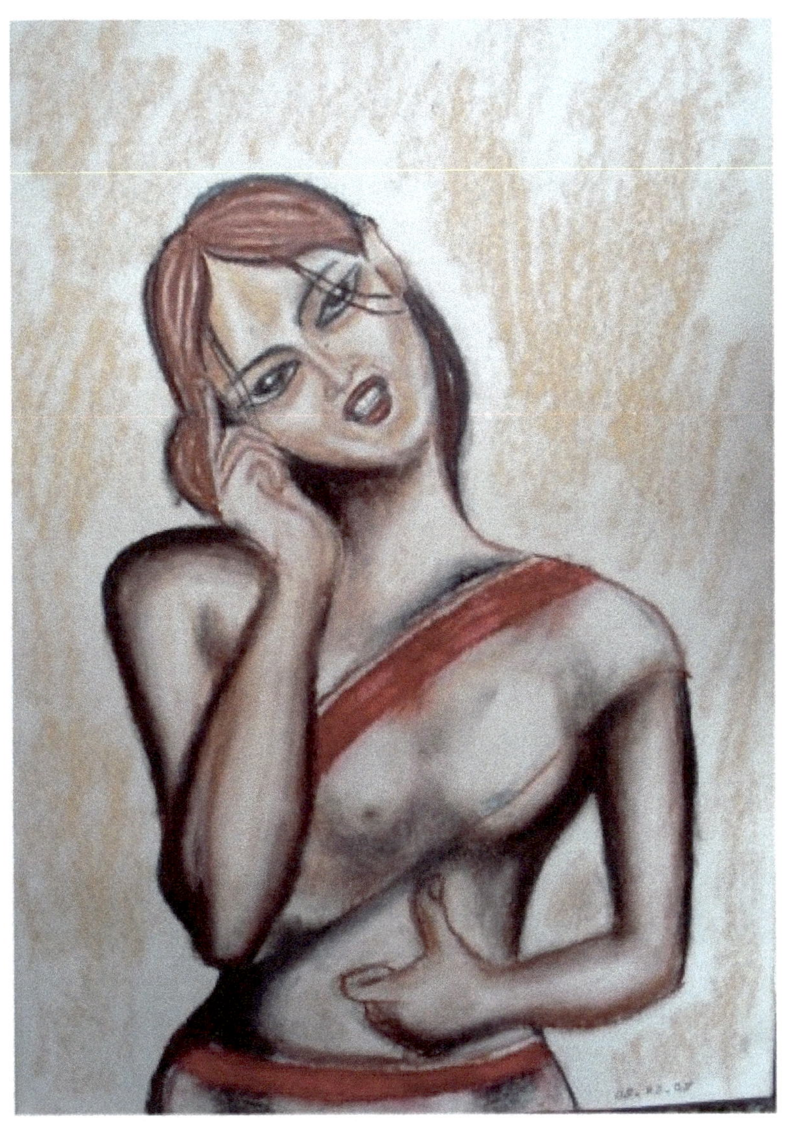

16 H X 10 W inches
Pastel on paper
July 2001

Cross-Border Love

Painted in stretched canvas! People divided our earth in separate countries with many cross-border lines. However, the LOVE between people living in cross-border countries tie them again, making a united world eventually. Here love wins against the cross-border separation.

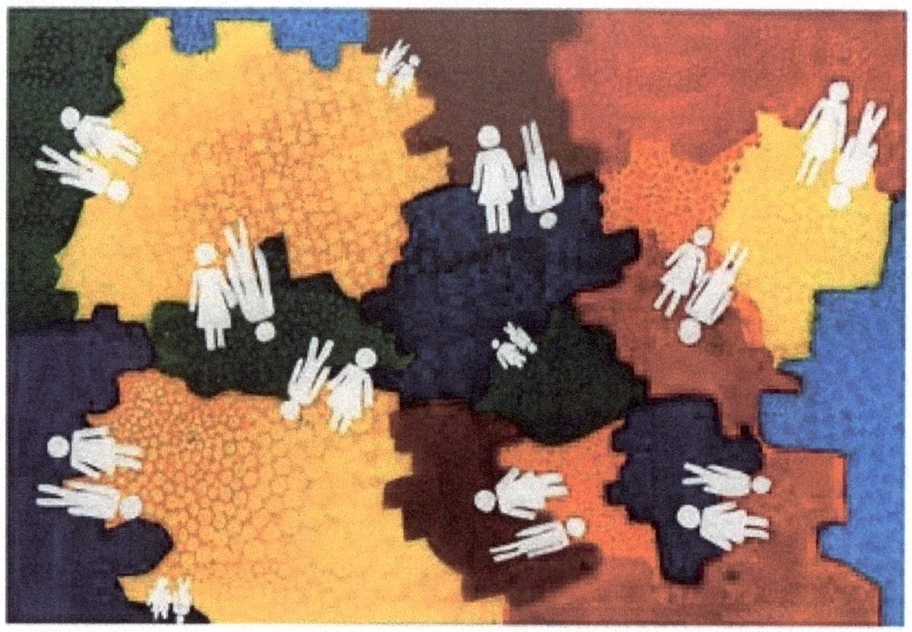

SIZE: 31.5 H x 47.2 W Inches
CATEGORY: painting
TECHNIQUE: acrylic
STYLE: abstract
SUPPORT: acrylic
YEAR: 2022

MARMAID (ONE-EYED LOVE)

SIZE 31.5 H x 47.2 W Inches
CATEGORY: painting
TECHNIQUE: acrylic
STYLE: abstract
SUPPORT: acrylic
YEAR: 2022

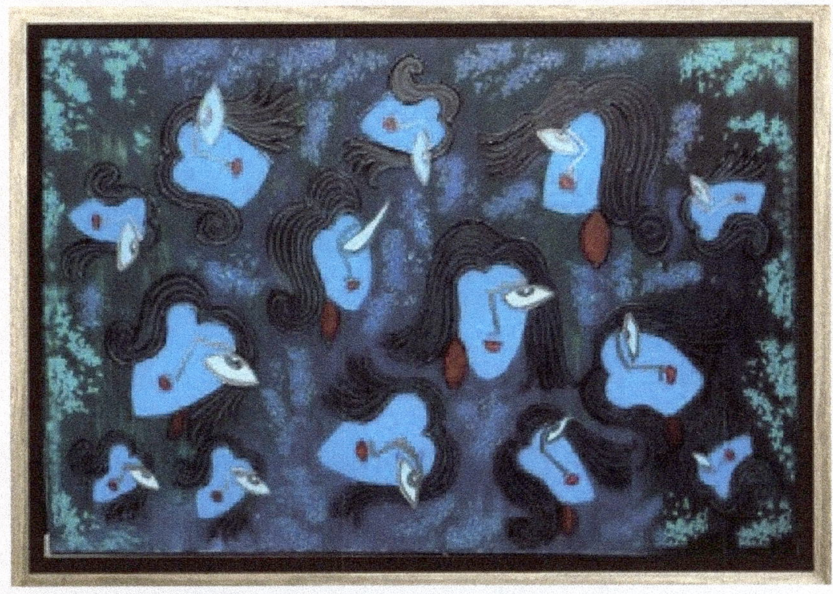

Painted on stretched canvas. Women are mothers. It is obvious that women always ready to sacrifice their own lives for their child, for their kids. Their 'one-eyed love' only can see their children/kids safety, but not their own!

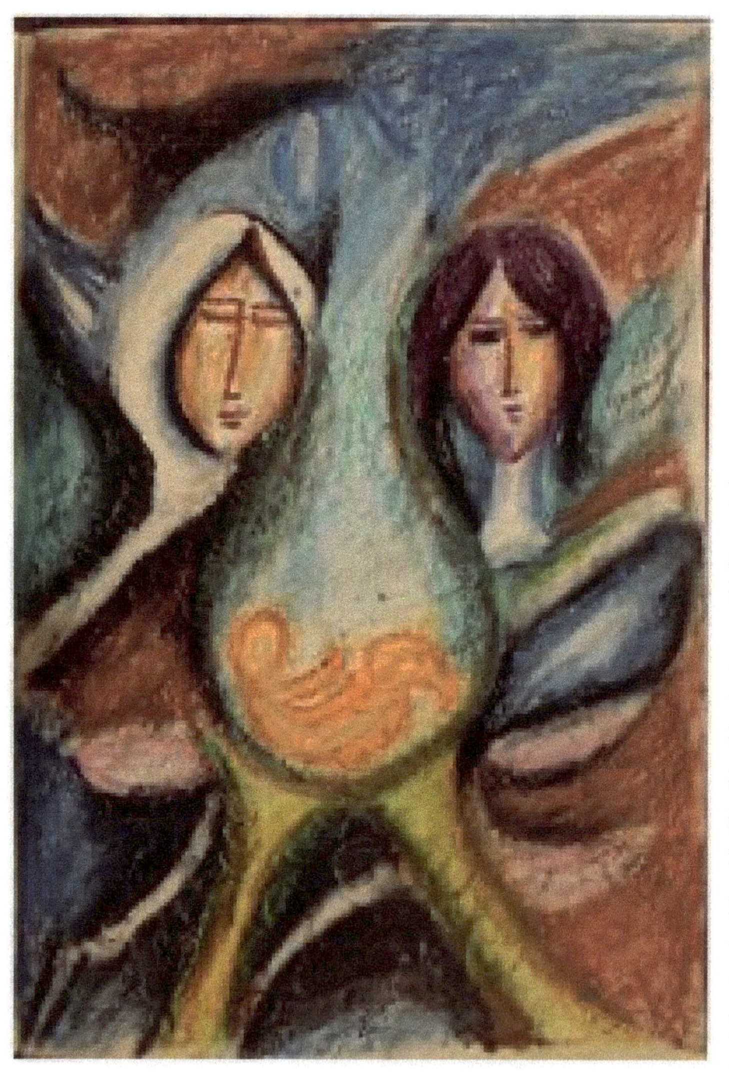

"Birth",
Media: Pastel Color,
Size: 10 X 16 inch,

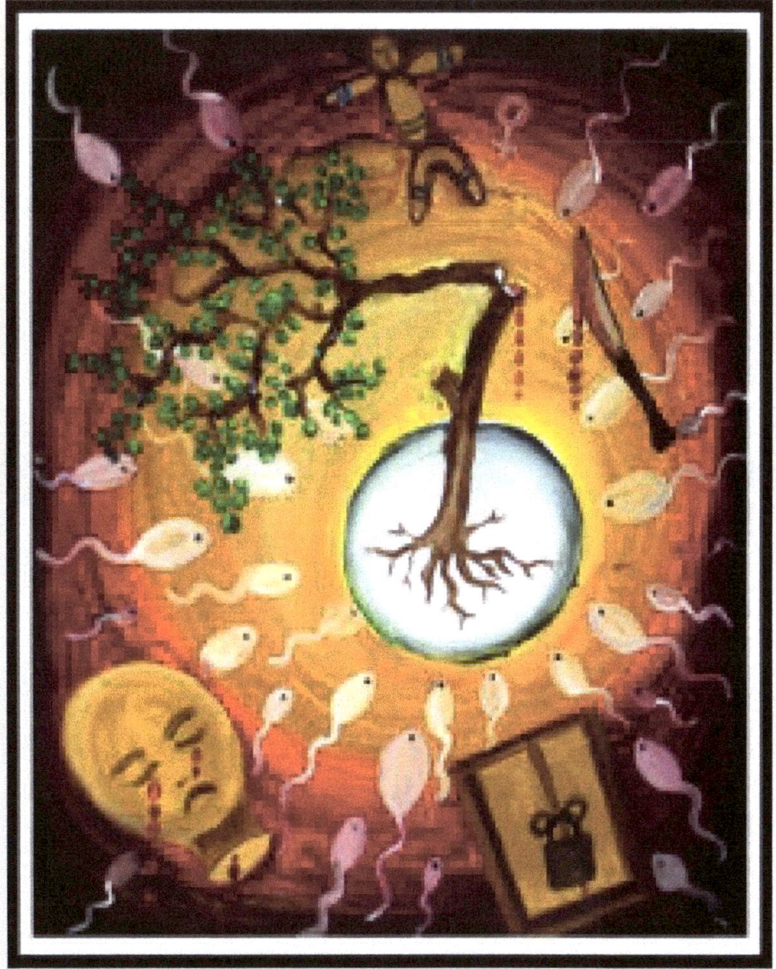

"Abortion",

Media: Oil Painting on board,

Size: 18 X 24 inch,

Date: August, 2010,

Premise: Ontario, Canada.

Exhibited on "Annual painting

Exhibition, in Toronto".

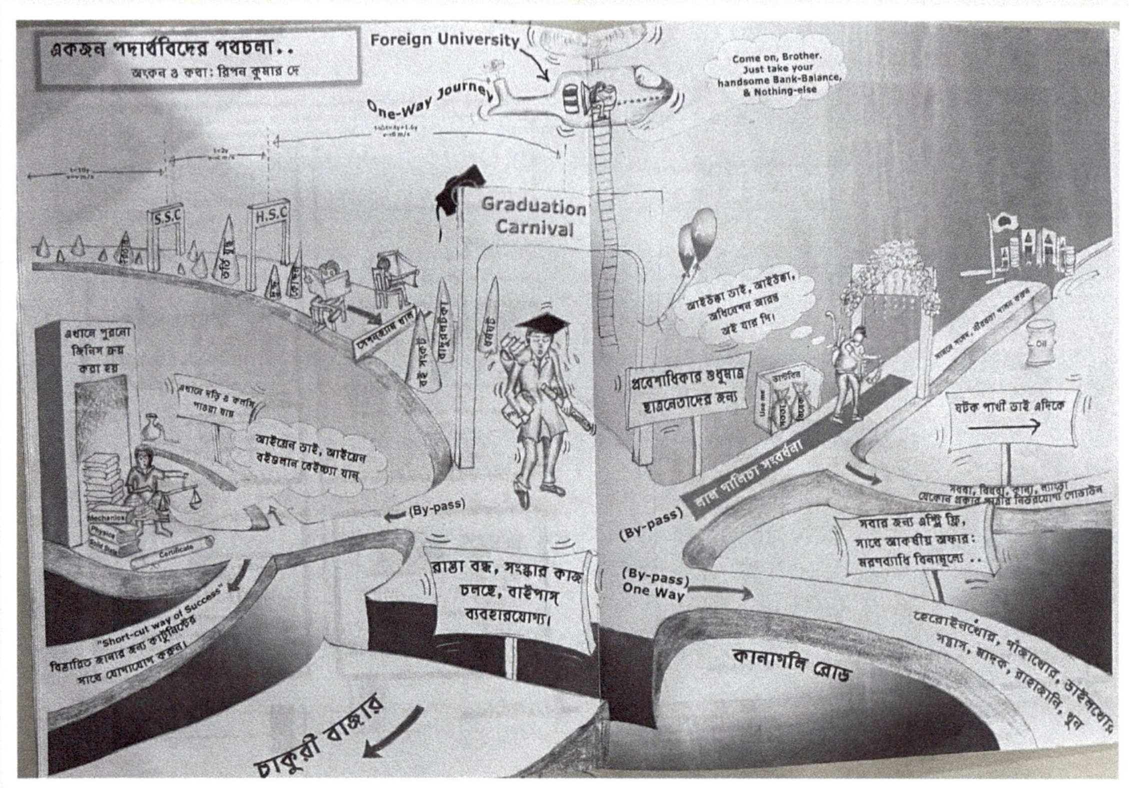

"A life of a physicist in

Bangladesh",

Media: Pen and paper

Size: 18 X 24 inch,

Date: August, 2010,

EXOTIC ARTWORKS

RIPON DEY

54